T0067187

Act as If:
Think It into Existence

Your Thoughts Create Your Reality

Author of "Why Am I Stuck?"
& Co-Author of "101 Great Ways To Improve Your Life"

Ehryck F. Gilmore Ch.

BALBOA.
PRESS
A DIVISION OF HAY HOUSE

Balboa Press books may be ordered through booksellers or by contacting:

Balboa Press
A Division of Hay House
1663 Liberty Drive
Bloomington, IN 47403
www.balboapress.com
1 (877) 407-4847

Because of the dynamic nature of the Internet, any web addresses or
links contained in this book may have changed since publication and
may no longer be valid. The views expressed in this work are solely those
of the author and do not necessarily reflect the views of the publisher,
and the publisher hereby disclaims any responsibility for them.

The author of this book does not dispense medical advice or prescribe the use
of any technique as a form of treatment for physical, emotional, or medical
problems without the advice of a physician, either directly or indirectly. The
intent of the author is only to offer information of a general nature to help
you in your quest for emotional and spiritual well-being. In the event you use
any of the information in this book for yourself, which is your constitutional
right, the author and the publisher assume no responsibility for your actions.

Any people depicted in stock imagery provided by Thinkstock are
models, and such images are being used for illustrative purposes only.
Certain stock imagery © Thinkstock.

Print information available on the last page.

ISBN: 978-1-5043-9108-5 (sc)
ISBN: 978-1-5043-9109-2 (e)

Balboa Press rev. date: 07/15/2020

Dedication

To **"All That Is,"** and everyone else
that supported the production of this book
physically, mentally and spiritually.

Lissa Woodson-Interior
Larry Gibson-book cover
Jeanne Ricks-music
Esther and Jerry Hicks,
J.Z. Knight,
Napoleon Hill,
Dr.Johnnie Colemon,
R.H.Jarrett,
Ernest Holmes,
Steve Strickland & Megan Mitchell: BMS Expo.
Behe-Jahe Williams-consultant
Thank You!

Much Universal Love & Energy, Ehryck F. Gilmore

Contents

I BEGIN
WHEN YOU BEGIN ...
I AM

Preface

What is "Act As If"?

The Question begs an answer!

Act As If: is to be proactive & not reactive.
Act As If: decisive & deliberate manifesting.
Act As If: to live a purposeful & passionate life.
Act As If: is to become confident & committed.
Act As If: is to thrive & not just live.
Act As If: is to go beyond *"What Is"*.

Is *"Act As If"* Magic? Undoubtedly, but the magic is also already in your mind. The easiest way to access this magic is to think of your **Thoughts** as things with the ability to brings objects into fruition. By being proactive, you can reprogram your conscious and subconscious mind by systematically using tenets of the **"Law of Attraction."**

Once you understand the Law Of Attraction's potential you will be able to embrace the "Act As If" technique. Then and only then you will be able to create and manifest all your lifelong desires on purpose. To "Act As If" is very similar to the concept, *"Whatever Happens In Vegas Stays in Vegas"* with which you create a new persona for the weekend. The **"Act As If"** technique is a two-part exercise, first in your mind, you see yourself experiencing your desire. Next, you physically conduct your behavior as if it already exists. If needed, you can also adopt a persona that you deem necessary to help you secure a particular job, career advancement, or for entertainment purposes that you want to experience. When you do incorporate an "Act As If" persona, however, it doesn't have to "stay in Vegas."

You can use this technique in your everyday life and become whoever or whatever you want for any duration of time required, regardless of social status and without judgment. However, people will judge, and some well-meaning friends will advise you to over-analyze your life and find the reason you are not successful. Out the other side of their mouth, they will scream, "you should be like Oprah, Obama, Madonna; you can win, you can become successful! Go for it all, and don't stop. The flip-side of living a full-throttle *"Go Big or Go Home"* life is to follow the familiar humdrum path of getting a good government job. A good cushy government job one that comes with a bountiful 401K and plenty of stagnation. It sounds a little confusing, but you do have a choice, and you can choose to exist or live and thrive.

"Stop the Madness!" Don't get

overwhelmed. Yes, you can revitalize, reenergize, and reimagine your life if you start with your dreams, passions, and goals because feelings ignite desire. And by actively visualizing and focusing decisively on what you want—a yearning for, to the point you will deliberately create and manifest in physical form. What you seek is seeking you and will match your new consciousness.

How? By reading self-help books, watching videos, reciting mantras, and practicing meditation? Well, yes! There are self-help books that are very reliable with useful information on how to change the negative way you think. However, rarely do they explain and give you instructions on how you can reprogram your mind and behavior to take control of your life. As with any self-help techniques, it's essential to proceed with caution before you realign and reprogram the Conscious and Subconscious Mind. But not to worry; deliberately recreating and reprogramming your life, requires no additional unique set of tools. Except, specifically, knowing, **"What do you want"** because nature abhors a vacuum.

Step one: you must be willing to change your non-productive behavior, habits, idiosyncrasy, and be open to taking decisive action. Even these seemingly difficult steps will take time, but it will lead you on the path to becoming an extraordinary person. **Step two:** Once you decide what you want, you have to change your beliefs and believe you can have it. **Step three:** write it down and be as specific and descriptive as you can from what you are seeing and feeling in your mind's eye.

Step four: is to Model *(mimic, imitate, pretend)* someone with those same great desirous attributes that you want to achieve. ***How?***, by exuding enough confidence to convince others and yourself that you are legitimate and qualified. A Role Model is not to be mistaken for a Mentor. A Mentor is an experienced guide, coach, or advisor within a company to teach you the ropes. One of those techniques used by corporate Mentors is the Carrot & Stick motivation approach. Which is specifically designed to help you reach your goals when used in conjunction with **"Act As If"** it will also trigger a similar behavior; to achieve your goals faster and deliberately.

Why, because it's a psychical incentive, much like a Vision board provides, resulting in **"EXPECTATION."** When you are expecting, you are in a state of anticipating, which is having a strong belief that something is going to happen or occur in the future, and you will be situated and ready to receive it. The key here is to know what you desire, what you exactly want, and how you plan to achieve it and expect it.

Should you Model someone? Yes, because its another exemplary technique in your metaphysical toolbox. But when "Acting As if," the idea is to come across as authentic and confident. Once you start "Acting As If" you have actually stepped outside of your comfort zone to create your **"I AM"** manifestation deliberately. Because I love the concept of **"ACT AS IF,"** which is the ability to take Thoughts, Feelings, Emotions, Imagination, and Vision along with Action to deliberately create anything you desirously want. I have attempted to capture the essence of "Act As If" and write in my vernacular, which is straight to the point, *"take no prisoners"* style, Beginner's Guide 101 and simplify the understanding for those who are new to this incredible phenomenon.

Is it "A Fake It Until You Make It" guide? **No!** More like "Faith It Until You Make It"! But in all reality, it's a **Feign it until you Feel it!"** the precursor to **Act As If.** However, it isn't about deceiving people for mischievous or illicit purposes, or saying you have the abilities or skills you don't. It is a catchphrase for a technique used to build confidence and change behavior.

Attempt it right now, smile, Smile, SMILE, do you feel how that changed your mood? Thats how simple it is to ActAs If. But, more importantly, this is an **"Act As If"** guide with techniques and exercises, to explain how anyone can easily use their Thoughts to alter their consciousness from being reactive to proactive. If you are proactive, you make things happen instead of waiting around for them to happen to you. To be clear the prefix pro- is *"in advance of, or beforehand."* Which means active is *"diligent, lively, and vigorous."* Therefore if you are proactive, you are ready before manifestation happens. The flip side is being reactive or always waiting for negative things to fall into your lap and materialize before responding.

The aforementioned is why a proactive person consistently feels like they have choices, and because of this, they make a decisive choice, while proudly owning it. Hence you are now deliberately creating, decisiveness at its best. Again, being reactive means that you don't take the initiative or make decisive, deliberate decisions in your life; you take what life dishes out to you.

In response, you act surprised and want to react to what happened to you, in certain instances, it's with pure positive actions, but usually, it is with a negative approach involving your hurt feelings.

As you read how to apply and work the "ActAs If" techniques throughout this book, they will consist of Metaphysical principles. And not to alienate anyone's religion or spiritual beliefs. I hope you will find inspiration in knowing that the **Law of Attraction** tenets can be found in many Biblical texts. In Proverbs 29:18 in the Bible expresses *"Where there is no vision, the people perish: but he that keepeth the **"Law,"** happy is he.* Another Bible version; *Where there is no vision, the people are unrestrained, but happy is he who keeps the **"Law."***

I CANNOT WANT IT
MORE THAN YOU . . .
SO SAYS THE
UNIVERSE

"You Cannot Move Forward With Your Foot On Someone Else's Throat."

CHAPTER 1

The Magic of your Mind

Who are you? What are you aware of? And What do you want? Let's start here. Why? Because if you don't know why you persistently focus on certain things, you won't become aware of how to move into a more productive environment. Where you place your attention is where your focus flows. Yet, almost everyone I have encountered has asked why their desire or goals do not come to fruition asap. They exclaim they are intelligent, knowledgeable, responsible, and good people. However, being a good person is nice, but not enough; you must consciously start putting into action the necessary work to change your life. Many people I know want to change their lives but find it difficult. In addition to wanting to be heard, they are consistently looking for someone to listen to their woes and to validate they are alive. Beyond that, they are seeking help to make the right choices and break old habitual thinking that has caused stress in their life.

The saving grace is you can transform your life; you can

change the channel simply by "Acting As If"—adopting a positive attitude and thinking Thoughts that can eventually lead you to manifest your desire. When you **"Act As If"** you will have the ability to explain and understand happenstances without using old platitudes such as "Luck."

LUCK: What is Luck? Basically escapism, a way to distract you from putting in the necessary work to reinforce your desire. Dictionaries say it's something good that happens by chance. Luck has nothing to do with what you are experiencing in life right now. Because you are already "Acting As if." Either you are deliberately creating and manifesting it or attracting it by default. The "by default" option means you are not aware, consciously, or mindful of the deficient choices you make in life.

AFRAID Of What? At some point in your life, unbeknownst to you, you had already mentally adopted the "Act As If" technique to live the American Dream. In doing so, your dreams, desires, and goals came to fruition by putting forth enough faith, belief, and a clear vision. Think back to when you were choosing your house, furniture, car, friends, schools, and career, those choices started as desirous visualizing. Through your imagination, you created the mental staging for the theater of your life. Without hesitation or fear, you knew, precisely what you wanted, focused your attention toward it and went after it. When you are scared of the unknown, you are only cheating yourself out of the chance to experience all the unexplored possibilities in life. Being afraid means, you have not taken the time to research that which you desire. The solution is to digest the new information in small enough chunks to turn *"what if"* it doesn't work in the negative to *"what if"* it does work-out beautifully, in the positive.

Whether you deliberately choose a proactive script for your life or haphazardly adopt one by default, eventually, you will consciously surmise it's easier and better, too, "ActAs If."

PARASITES & Vampires: When People tell you who they are…They're not joking! Sooner rather than later, they will have a Freudian slip. You don't have time to waste, stay reliant, vehemently focus on your desire; there will always be people who come to your house, workplace, etc., to ask for help. These wanderers are considered hanger Onners or parasites—not giving but always taking, basically exploiting any situation for their benefit.

Then there are Vampires, those spiritually unfed people whom you interact with every day and are still craving for your attention. If you don't give them attention freely, they will get it from another. The classic Tear or Fear technique refers to tears for sympathy or intimidation is when a person is willing to scream and yell until you submit to their demands.

CONFIDENCE: Unpretentiously let go of the melodrama because being consciously aware and "Acting As If" can now change your behavior. And by building enough confidence, you will be able to remove yourself from any energy-draining unproductive situations. But first, you must

decide whether you desire to be in a proactive environment with like-minded people. It is with this confidence in yourself and your capacity to learn while **Acting AS If** that is the key. If you want something badly enough, you'll learn how to do it. How, by getting into character or alignment and doing enough **"I Am"** self work for your subconscious mind to create the pattern. How long depends on what it is you need to learn, how you practice, and the effort you put in its called consistency." Basically, it is about changing your behavior to one of confidence. Therefore "Act As If" until you feel like you have succeeded in our task.

Acting allows your subconscious mind to adjust to new information and accept the subtle changes.

While you could term this a **"Act As If"** technique, even though it's really an expression of confidence. This approach is about convincing yourself that there really isn't anything to fret about. Adding to this, it actually increases natural confidence and, in turn, one becomes more confident in their behavior. In circumstances where the challenge truly is lack of confidence, it can actually help to "Act As If. Thus to confidently change yourself, to liberate yourself from the entrenched or erroneously acquired behaviors to the one that is wanted, You must reprogram your mind. By "Acting As If" while applying the preferable behavior consistently, you are teaching your subconscious mind to develop a new type of behavior. By imitating confidence, competence, and an having positive mindset, a person can achieve those characteristics in real life.

As stated before, "Acting As If" becomes much easier when you surround yourself with people who you desire to be like and emulate. Researchers have discovered that just "Acting" a certain way allows your brain to experiment with alternative methods of thinking.

Be that as it may, you can't just **"Act As If"** part of the time. You must immerse yourself and remain in character in all circumstances. "Acting As If" needs to become a daily occurrence, part of your psyche, and actions. If you want to be a millionaire, then act like one. Exposure yourself to people who are more successful than you. Dress, do, and think like one, expand your vocabulary.

Take decisive action instead of just talking. It's about making the right deliberate decisions in order to achieve all of your desires, dreams, and goals. We become like the people we affiliate with, and that's why winners are attracted to winners. If you believe that you deserve something, your thoughts slowly align to it. Then your actions align with the Universe. The power of emotions, thoughts and beliefs drive your actions. As a consequence good, bad, or indifferent your actions are driven naturally by your thoughts and feelings.

CONSPIRE: The Universe does not conspire against you. Metaphysically speaking, people usually get exactly what they ask for, but most of the time, they don't ask specifically for what they want. In some cases, it takes a lot of adversity and difficulties to get one to acknowledge something they desire.

Likewise, the Universe does not conspire to make you do anything at all. You deliberately decided to do what you wanted to do because it satisfied a need you had at the time. It is apparent, you can be persuaded by others to act on their interest, but that is still not the Universe coercing you. Be honest with yourself; your wrong decisions and bad results doesn't mean the Universe is conspiring against you. Its because you are vibrating and emitting deficient energy and, in return, attracting adversity. Long story short a case of self-sabotage.

It's like Shadow-boxing and beating yourself up to prove you're a winner. Unbeknownst to you, in reality, it's you actively or passively, taking steps mentally, and physically, to prevent yourself from reaching your desires, dreams, or goals. Essential getting in your own way, procrastinating, with an absence of obvious motivation, overindulgence in every category, and repeated incidents of conflict within your daily existence, creating an unnecessary mess.

Stop sabotaging yourself, it's in your mindset to align with the Universe. If you work within the principles of the spiritual laws, then the Universe will reciprocate. The Law Of Attraction works if you work it. Take responsibility for all your choices and actions.

The Universe is merely too vast to be concerned about conspiring against you; it just matches your vibration. Instead of looking to blame the Universe for your indecisive actions. Make a commitment change your Thoughts to ones that are deliberate, decisive, and definite, then you can take responsibility for the positive outcomes as well.

COMMITMENT: And that takes dedicating yourself to your desire, dream, or goal. Before you commit, think carefully, decide if what you want is a desire, or is just a fanciful wish. Stating to others what you want and taking no action is just window dressing to make oneself look like they are achieving success. Because a commitment obligates you to do something, it is a promise or agreement, and most can't keep that accountability. When you say altruistically, you desire to save the world and help others make sure you are decisive. You must have a clear picture and know exactly how you plan to achieve this level of benevolence in your mind first. Because when you do diligence and commit to yourself fist, it helps you commit to others.

"Regardless of who you are or what you have been, you can be what you want to be.—
W. Clement Stone

I See You, I Hear You,
But You Don't Hear
Me…Because of All
the Imaginary Noise,
Confusion, and Chaos in
Your Life… Close Your
Eyes & Open Your Mind,
I Will Be With You A
1000 times & Then…
I AM

CHAPTER 2

Universal Laws

Have you ever wondered how the rich get richer or how those who speak of sickness never seem to get well? Maybe you have even wondered how those who appear to have nothing can be so generous, and those with overflowing abundance can be so unenlightened. It's through their Thoughts, **yes!**Thoughts.

What you think about has the power to create the object or situation you concentrate the most on. I know you have watched for years how men and women you thought were less deserving receive gifts of abundance. However, those people were no less worthy than you; what they possessed was a strong desire to achieve success and a burning ambition to live their life passionately.

The difference between successful people and your desirous self is that successful individuals are sending out focused, **Deliberate Thoughts** into the Universe — Concentrated Thoughts to attract what they are seeking. Specifically, knowing precisely what you want is undoubtedly the first step towards achieving it, and this does not include vague wishing. Daydreaming and hoping does not include enough focused energy to bring your desire to fruition. The task of creating your passion and bringing forth that desire involves putting your imagination to work. You must have a clear picture of what you want and be willing to do the necessary work. You can successfully change your life even if it involves changing your environment to accomplish the task.

The primary spiritual principles of the Law of Attraction can also be affirmed in the teachings of many cultural and religious groups. The Bible says, ***"It is through thinking that man forms that which he has in life."***(Proverbs 23:7).

A phrase that is strikingly similar to the universal Law of Attraction is *"That which you are craving is developing, evolving, and materializing."* Is this a Secret? Yes, but only to those who have not heard about the Universal Laws.

One of these laws is the incomparable, immutable **Law of Attraction.** The great masters envisioned one day there would be spiritual, orderly, enlightened societies illuminated by the sharing of unmitigated thought. How might this be done?

By deliberately creating and developing one's internal computer, which is your conscious mind. It is also achieved by your consciousness and how you are feeling, in a given moment in time. All the "Spiritual laws" always work. The most challenging part of acknowledging and accepting the truth of what the Law of Attraction has to offer is realizing that every single one of your decisions in life, negative and positive, have been shaped by you alone through previous decisive thoughts. There might be instances where we don't fully know how the Universal Laws work, and there are times people don't understand what the Law Of Attraction actually states or how to implement it.

Implementing the Law, right way consists of choosing deliberate positive thoughts, which make an enormous impact. Use Affirmations and Visualization, journaling, and attaching a list of your goals on your vision board where you can view it every day does increase its probability of making it manifest sooner rather than later. The main reason the Law is able to bring your desire to fruition with specificity is that the Universe mirrors your feelings and deliberate thoughts; and responds precisely by matching your vibrations as they were received but returning them in physical form.

A big challenge for you now, is in the implementation of these spiritual principles into your Subconscious mind. Which is the part of your brain whose job it is to store beliefs, emotionalized thoughts, and affect behavior, basically a large memory bank. Besides working as a vault, it permanently saves everything that ever happens to you in life. However, your Conscious mind rules the Subconscious mind, but it's the rote subconscious mind without your awareness that sends the vibrations to the Universe.

Thus, the most important prerequisite is to make the Law of Attraction work deliberately asap, and that starts with downloading your subconscious mind with decisive thoughts.Which, in turn, will accelerate and send positive vibrations to the Universe, eventually returning to you a physical equivalent, of said desire.

The Law of Attraction is really that simple if you can hold onto an idea and see it for yourself in the mind's eye, you can make it yours to have; of course it takes some mental and physical effort on your part.

There can be no doubt the Law of Attraction is your ability to attract into your lives whatever you are intentionally focusing upon.

It is understood irrespective of age, nationality, or religious belief, you are easily influenced by the Law Of Attraction, which governs the Universe, in conjunction with the other 12 commonly known Spiritual Laws. But it is the Law of Attraction that utilizes the power of the Conscious and Subconscious mind to interpret and transform whatever is in your thoughts and materialize them into reality. Broadly speaking, all Deliberate, Decisive Thoughts turn into things ultimately at some point.

Unfortunately, so many of us are **Stuck** and still unaware of all the possibilities and the potential locked deep within us. That is why the Universal Laws, including The Law Of Attraction, was necessary to create a learning utopia of enlightenment on Earth. And now Quantum Physics is catching up to bear witness to what metaphysicians have all ways known about the Spiritual Laws, and that is;

Thought + Desire + Emotion + Visualization + Belief + Expectancy = Manifestation!

Now, the secret of the Universe's Law of Attraction's power has finally been revealed. After centuries of being co-opted, manipulated, and diluted by the intelligentsia for selfish gains.

Now, imagine, if you will, a beautiful exotic bird escaping from its gilded cage, flying high and unimpeded; so is the realigning of the human experience to the Universe as people become anew manifesting with the help of this spiritual Law. Because when it's all said and done, your "Action speaks louder than words," take action, and let the things you do show your true intentions and feelings.

Ergo escape your gilded mental cage, aka your comfort zone the Universe is limitless, and your imagination is boundless.

"It Works If You Work It!" -Dr. Johnnie Colemon,

Muse On:

1. Act As If: to pretend or Role Model until you have absorbed the essence of confidence.
2. Remember, no one can want your desire or goal for you more than you want it for yourself.
3. Ask yourself: When will I become responsible for my decisions?
4. Ask yourself: When will I know that I can manifest my desire?
5. Ask yourself: Why Am I so loved?
6. Ask yourself: In what ways Am I consciously aware?
7. Ask yourself: Why am I so excited today?

Affirmation: I Am ready

BEYOND
YOUR THOUGHTS LIVES
ANOTHER WORLD

CHAPTER 3

The Law of Attraction & How It Works

How does the Law of Attraction work? First, the Law is impartial and impersonal depending on your Thoughts; it can work for you or against you. The Law of Attraction is explicitly designed to send you more of whatever you passionately think about without any judgment. "Spiritually speaking," once you are crystal clear about what you want, the Law beckons, *"what would you have me manifest?"*

How simple is that?

Too simple, you say? Then, let's examine how choosing clear Thoughts with "Positive Intention" works. As we already know, everything in the Universe is m of energy, so your cells, neurons, and the very atoms of your body are constantly vibrating. Even your thoughts are made up of microscopic energy particles that have magnetic properties, attracting like particles, clinging together to create a bigger Thought-form.

Amazingly, the vibrational string between thought pattern energies begins to create and reinforce connections. Think of a spider spinning its web, each silky thread stretching and building on the other, becoming stronger and harder. The same concept applies to those Thought substances. Those streams of thoughts have the same vibrational energy, which creates a frequency wave to attract and make a connection. When this happens, we begin to attract our desire as our focused energy connects to an equal vibration of the object or another person. But before manifestation can become activated, you must have a clear understanding of utilizing the Law Of Attraction, primarily that Thoughts are living things.

Yes, just like apples, oranges, bees, animals, and trees, thoughts are living things. Understanding the concept takes a tremendous leap of faith -- even though you cannot see gravity, you still believe it exists. And having that belief in something invisible even when it does not line up with your core beliefs puts your mind in control. If you knew how powerful your **"Thoughts"** were, you would be mesmerized at how they create the desire of your dreams. The magic consists of using your imagination with a mixture of Clear, Focused Thoughts, Visualizing, and Emotion with an intense yearning to manifest. This enthusiasm is how the Universe matches your desires and the way it always has been achieved.

On the opposite side of pure positive, deliberate energy is negative stuff. The Law of Attraction does not distinguish between positive and negative energy, so **"please,"** remain in a state of anticipation. You may think you can avoid your negative style of thinking, but you can not. Negative thoughts will broadcast that they are apart of your life, continually reappearing, causing havoc at different points of celebration until you eradicate or supersede them with positive ideas that are in your best interest. Because negativity also has the power to bring to the unconscious mind more Defeatist Thoughts to easily manipulated and formed into a substance for fruition. Therefore, do not spend your time analyzing Pessimistic Thoughts, allowing uncontrollable emotions to seep into your mind. All that doubt, second-guessing, uncertainty, and negativity does is slow down your manifestation. On the other hand, when you choose deliberate recurring Positive Thoughts, they automatically start the maturation of your desire. Once those Focused Thoughts receive the needed Emotion, fruition is not far behind.

Serendipity? No, it's your aware consciousness and the strength of your vibrations, ones emitting full-bodied descriptive energy, causing microscopic energy particles to stick to things you want to attract as if you were a lure and magnet. As the energy reconfigures in the Universe, it returns your desire in material form. Also, if you believe you have the ability to visualize clear, positive images in your mind, your attraction will be nothing but successful. However any spiritual laws, improperly used will bring unsatisfactory results.

Whew! That's a brief description of the Law of Attraction's omnipotent power, but that's plenty to wrap your mind around. Now understanding how to use the Law, if you change what you focus on, you can Deliberately Create and get what you want. But don't focus on what you do not want, because ***"What You Resist Persists"*** It would be best if you watched what you place your focus on. Because what people focus on, they ultimately move towards. And by being consciously aware mentally, you hold your attention on your desire with clarity, while taking action to bring it to fruition. Focus effortlessly also on only where you want to go using your imagination and see yourself having it, being, and doing it.

When you analyze what's behind this infinite, invisible magic, you will see it's your consciousness, mindfulness, I Am-ness, and the Universe conspiring to bring forth your desire. By virtue of all those Desirous Thoughts, you experience during the day and then stockpiled in your subconscious.

Where do all of those Thoughts of things, experiences, and wishes get stored? They're kept in the repository of your subconscious mind until enough sufficient thoughts with similar data accumulate.

Now, visualize a picture of your mind as a commercial bank able to perform several types of financial services. Start with your awakening, responsive, and self-aware Conscious Mind acting as a bank teller—greeting you, checking your identification, and taking your deposits *(Thoughts)*. Finally, the teller sends information to bookkeeping — this where all transactions are sorted and tallied at the end of the day. Next, the Subconscious Mind, which is unaware, is where previous perused information is saved and operates as a bank vault. Finally, when enough similar thoughts combined with enough emotion are deposited in your account *(subconscious mind)*, they consolidate.

With a potent frequency, they send a signal to the Universe to start the materialization of your desire. Once manifestation has completed, you can make an initial withdrawal from an ATM, metaphorically speaking. However, you can only withdraw what you have deposited, so be extra mindful, specific, deliberate, and purposeful.

There is one thing you should never forget; your **Focused Thoughts** are the backbone of creating and transforming your desire into a highly anticipated physical form equivalent. And the only way you will not succeed in bringing your desire to fruition is if you delay or hesitate not being clear about your desire and hoping for better options.

People often procrastinate because they're afraid of failing at the chore that they need to accomplish. This fear of failure can trigger procrastination in a varied number of ways. One being, not being able to make hard deceives choices another being avoidance, which is not facing a challenge by scheduling it for a later date and then rescheduling. And yet another tactic is not getting started on what you want, before all else, by placing it after breakfast, lunch, dinner, kids, career, internet, concert, soap operas, baseball, archery, and yachting, but at the end of the day, it's nothing but **FEAR** masquerading as excuses. Fear is just not knowing enough about the subject to make a rash judgment call. Instead of delving deeper into the subject, to uncover enlightenment you're apt to put it off for an extended period of time not wanting to exert any brainpower on a daunting task. You must be clear about what you want without fear but with clarity; because you will get **STUCK** and overthinking your desired outcome. Instead, focus on "what you want", not on the task of how you are going to bring it into Existence. After you get focused, visualize in your mind your desire all the smells, textures, and sights feel them as if it is happening in the now. See yourself being motivated by knowing you will be experiencing the manifestation of your desire the physical reward for believing in yourself.

Start, now immediately asking yourself the unambiguous questions that will help you expedite your desire. Questions such as, *How quickly will I learn the skills necessary to focus clearly?*, *How come I Am so abundant? Why Am I so Blessed?* In addition to *How come I Am so gifted? How can I become more deliberately decisive in my choices?*

Make your limitless mind do the research, and it will automatically once those questions are broached.

Calibrate get in synced and let your subconscious mind work in the capacity of a data memory bank, matching those questions to specific past experiences, making it possible for you to have succinct impactful answers. Calibration can help remind you and define what you want and bring about, which is a very remarkable achievement.

When you Calibrate, you achieve the feeling of being in alignment with your higher self. When you Calibrate with others and negative situations, you will feel like you are walking around in a daze, unable to get clarity on any given subject. Hence focus on how you wish to feel until you're eventually in that feeling space. This way, you can also explore the expansionism of your freedom; in such, you will be happy all the time whether your desire happens now or later. Calibrating, is allowing that pure positive energy to flow into your Vortex, also known as your spiritual data memory bank, and the Universe will understand this is who you are and send you more of what you are vibrating because this is who you are!

Albert Einstein said in essence, *"Everything is energy and that's all is to it. Match the frequency of the reality you want, and you cannot help but get that reality".*

Ruminate:

1. What do you desire?
2. What will that do for you?
3. Are you asking yourself the right questions?
4. Ask yourself: How can I manifest my desire?
5. Ask yourself : In what way can I become more consciously aware and appreciate the process?
6. Ask yourself: When will I notice that I Am more Confident?
7. Ask yourself: How can I become more abundant?

Affirmation: I Am worthy.

WHEN YOU DREAM,
DESIRE
THE WHOLE

CHAPTER 4

Mastering The Techniques of the Law of Attraction

Let me emphasize that you must become proficient in Visualization and master the techniques because The Law of Attraction does not negotiate. The Law doesn't even distinguish between positive or negative deeds and remains neutral on thoughts; it is immutable. The Law responds to the state of your consciousness at this moment. The Law also acknowledges your point of focus primarily where you're projecting your thoughts. Again, your thoughts must be focused, clear, and exact to emit enough energy to create a strong vibrational signal into the universe.

In addition to circumventing any previously perused passionless data, you must be mindful of your positive intent. The daydreams and wishes that are stored neatly away without much emotion in the back of your subconscious mind.

Waiting on similar thoughts with enough emotion turns

the incubating wishes into a positive intent. Whether they are negative thoughts or positive ones, the Law of Attraction responds by matching those thoughts accordingly.

You may think you need total compliance from the other party to make your desire manifest essentially, it is your thoughts that create your reality, nothing more and nothing less, and everyone is on equal footing when they **"Think it into Existence."** As a result of your past thoughts—good, bad, or indifferent —you are responding to previous thoughts in real-time. Because for every idea/action, there is a consequence and reaction thus must be played out. Some call it Karma, and others call it the Law Of Cause and Effect, however, *"you reap what you sow." (Galatians 6:7-8)*

Yes, there is social, ethnic, and cultural consciousness tied to your core belief system. And your beliefs are nothing more than a security blanket for you; they give you a feeling of confidence. Please don't get me wrong beliefs are powerful, but be cautious about what you believe in and what you put your faith in, mainly when it comes to yourself.

Ironically, the Law of Attraction doesn't take any of those ideologies into consideration—no exceptions.

But here's good news, thoughts are trained, and beliefs are learned, which means you can reprogram your mind to accept new ones and unlearn unproductive ones.

Therefore, restrain from referring to and relying on pessimistic core beliefs that have you stuck in a vortex of unhealthy thoughts, including ones with uncertainty, unhappiness, or unworthiness. It about using your conscious awareness, visualization, and mental acuity to change any negative and limiting beliefs you entertain. You have the power and the purposefulness to plow right through your opposing thoughts and the unfavorable environment in which you find yourself without exception. The Universal Laws are sagacious, robust, and replete.

Now, if you can wrap your mind around this Universal concept, ***"What You Think About You Bring About,"*** a cautionary quote to be selective about what you say, what you do, what you give your attention to, and who you spend your time with because what you think about you do bring about. In essence, "What you think, you become. What you feel, you attract, and What you imagine, you create."

Now you should be able to appreciate this untapped unlimited in potential Law of Attraction.

How does the Law work? The Law of Attraction attracts thoughts, ideas, people, situations, and circumstances towards you like a magnet.

Your Thoughts determine your desires. Essentially, *"Like always attracts like."* But there are two distinct ways the Law works to your advantage. When you think about an object that has caught your attention consistently and start feeling emotional about it unbeknownst to you, this is the beginning of creating your desire. The other way is using affirmations to knowingly downloading desirous specific subliminal thoughts into your subconscious mind also through visualization to create deliberately. Again, the Law of Attraction isn't just about thinking something into existence and then possessing it. It's about your thoughts, your predominant thoughts, feelings, and beliefs, which all must be in harmony with your desire. **A Thought, is the act of thinking.**

A Thought is an idea, an image, a sound, and even an emotional feeling that arises from the brain.

Case in point, have you ever observed when good people become depressed and confused, or who are accident-prone regularly suffer from *dis-eases*?

It is because they have attracted the experience or situation into their lives either directly or by default. Yes, default, by failing to remain mindful at any given time and not being also consciously aware of the negative/non-positive choices you are making at any given point in time. Notice I said dis-ease? When the soul is not at ease, it will show its dissatisfaction in your life. Nature Abhors a Vacuum of any kind. *As a man thinks in his heart, so is he – Proverbs 23:7*

Here's some great news--everyone is on equal footing because you can change your destiny. You can also create the reality of your desires by changing your Thoughts and the way you Feel. Yes, it can change your perspective, expectation, and manifestation, bringing you better health, wealth, and success.

So, it would help if you watched how you spend your time interacting with certain outside stimuli that will mentally cause you to have chemical reactions, in turn, ignite an array of feelings controlled and uncontrollable.

And then depending on how much emotional energy you expend on the issue denotes whether it will drain your mental psyche. Believe it, or not your emotions dictate how you stand.

When you are happy, you look up, walking with a strut, and when you are sad, depressed, your shoulders slump over your head hangs down, and you look towards the ground. Yes, emotions can Leave you physically dis-eased; it's all about feeling good, grateful, and appreciative.

Again, I know there is social, ethnic, and cultural consciousness that is woven into issues as well, but most of these are ingrained in your core belief system. Because core beliefs are so strongly-held, unyielding, and inflexible, we regularly refer back to them to get additional information on a new situation ignoring new information that contradicts it.

Nevertheless, if you chose to bring those biased, narrow-minded, dogmatic perspectives into a positive situation, negativity will start vibrating; at the frequency of unbridled pessimism.

Negativity can simultaneously affect anyone or anything within its path, causing pandemonium similar to a Tornadic vortex but with erratic emotions.

This invisible and impassioned force of cynicism has enough energy to cause one to blame others for slights, slip-ups, or misunderstandings.

Likewise, skepticism can cause others around you to

label your actions as complicated or just plain unfriendly. But when you are in alignment with positive core beliefs, you automatically know it–its when you received an unexpected gift and proclaimed that you had been "blessed." It's obvious your belief system is based on faith, and you are a person able to accept the unexpected. Positivity is a state of mind, and if you believe in your heart that you are good enough, then you will continue to see things in your world that reaffirm that belief by practicing gratitude. In fact, having unshakable positive beliefs is important because it leads to Self-beliefs' faith in your self-worth, confidence in your abilities, and belief that you are deserving of prosperity that you desire.

"You cannot shake hands with a clenched fist"— Mahatma Gandhi

It is essential to understand just how the Law Of Attraction works because there is no haven from this Law; it is infinite. This visible force is always working relentlessly to bring you more of what you are thinking and feeling.

Unfortunately, most of us go throughout the day without giving much consideration to our thoughts.

It would be best if you became consciously aware besides pay attention to where you focus thought. When you are focused, you are deliberately observing or thinking about something you want to experience.

It's very much like when you become so focused on a idea and end up at home after a hard day at work, not knowing which streets you took to get there, but somehow, you made it.

Nevertheless, Positive Thoughts alone are not enough to proceed to the next level; it takes decisive action. It also requires visualization, staying focused, and aligning your feelings with the object of your desire.

Without clear, concise, Deliberate Thoughts, you automatically lay the groundwork for attracting negative experiences and chaotic conditions.

Attraction by default, again, is defined as making negative non-positive choices or making no choice and following another directive mindlessly. When you are in this state of confusion, its usually brought on by stress, exhaustion, and sleeplessness. During this state, however, is when you are" **Attracting by Default."**

When this happens, seemingly, you are not consciously aware. More specifically, you can't stay focused.

Where you direct your attention is where your energy is going. To be a deliberate creator, you must not allow outside forces to take over your consciousness.

Again, if this happens, it will undoubtedly weaken your resolution and dilute Positive Thoughts. Remember, *"if you're not making decisions for your life —situation, others will make them for you."* In other words, your indecision is still deciding. Decide now; you will become a master at focused, Positive Thoughts and not attract by default.

Now you want to know what happens when bad things happen to good people? In essence, it's because these superb people have somehow attracted by default this crummy experience to their life.

You attract to yourself that which you are thinking about, but if your mind is on auto-pilot, anything can change your streams of Positive Thoughts.

You may be thinking, ***"Oh, this mumbo jumbo can't be real, precisely what are you saying?"*** I know this sounds a little avant-garde, non-traditional, but this Law of Attraction states you will receive an earthly equivalent of what you are vibrating *(focused Deliberate Thoughts with emotion),* no more and no less. When you have only wishful unclear thoughts, the saying goes:

"Be careful what you wish for because you just might get it" *(unfocused, unpredictable thoughts lacking emotions).* Thought always proceeds form, so you need to remember that Focus Thought always tends to manifest itself in material form.

You can't resign from life, and you can't escape Universal Laws because they are not human-made laws that dictate moral behavior standards and rules that govern human behavior. Those human-made laws we all agreed upon by the majority of us who believe in right or wrong and have a moral compass. Universal Laws are more akin to Natural Laws, which encompasses one's desire for life, liberty, and the pursuit of happiness. Being a Universal spiritual law, The Law of Attraction, will, in no way, be regulated, compromised, or adjudicated in a courtroom.

The Law Of Attraction is about honing your creative, deliberate thoughts to create your future life in the now. The Law of Attraction does not dictate to you what to think or when to think, whether it is a negative or positive thought.

Here's more great news: there is no one in the heavens, judging the outcome of any of your experiences or the choices you're making for your life. The options to create a life beyond your wildest dreams are endless and as large as you can make them.

How do you become conscious of your choices? You can achieve this by being aware, mindful, and by researching and ultimately becoming immersed in understanding the Law of Attraction.

When I speak of the Law, I am specifically talking about the **Law of Attraction.** However, there are approximately twelve metaphysically formulated Universal Spiritual Laws that coincide with human enlightenment. Here is a brief overview of the most popular laws:

The Law of Cause and Effect: Every action has a reaction even if it comes from someone else. *(Nothing happens by chance, you are responsible for what goes on in your life, you reap what you sow.)*

Law Of Compensation: You are compensated with blessings and abundance when you do good deeds *(time, money, sharing, caring, gifting and blessing others).*

Law of Oneness: We are all connected *(what we say, do, and think, affects each other)*.

Law of Action: Putting Thoughts into action, taking the necessary steps to move you forward to change your vibrations, *(Engaging in activities that move you towards your dreams, desire, and goals)*.

Law of Vibration: Everything in the Universe vibrates, *(sound, light, thoughts, emotion, words, Plants, animals all have a frequency in which it communicates)*.

Law of Relativity: There are challenges in Life. *(This law wants you to look at how others are struggling to gain perspective of your shortcomings.)*

Law Of Polarity: Everything has an opposite and can't live without it, *(Success-Failure)*.

Law of Gratitude: Grateful for all we have, *(receive to appreciate to the universe and others for help making things happen)*.

Law Of Rhythm: Everything in the universe has a rhythm, *(the seasons changing, life is ebb and flow, different stages)*.

Law of Perpetual Transmutation: Everything is changing, nothing or no one remains the same, *(you are constantly changing under unending renovation for the good or bad)*.

Law Of Gender: Everything in nature is both male and female energy, *(both required to exist)*.

The Law of Karma: The sum of a person's previous existence actions as well as the results of actions taken now. It is good intention equals good Karma, and bad intentions will return bad Karma; what one did yesterday will impact tomorrow.

Cause and Effect: In essence, with Cause and Effect there is no one to blame, but oneself's for what happens to them because they caused it with their previous actions.

The Law of Responsibility: The ability to respond to any individual or situation at any given time. Every person is immensely powerful and responsible for their feelings; and their destiny. The more responsible one is, the more one empowers oneself from being a victim.

Justification: Providing a adequate reason or excuse for something done or not completed, a person one who is a justifier, states it to be accurate, standing in conviction, self-validation. Its an explanation as to why your belief is a true one. Essentially when you can no longer defend your poor choices, you offer a justification. If you trace the fruit of your un-deliberate choices back to its source, you will see the formation of its unstable roots, actually came from the malnutrition seeds you planted, which were your toxic core beliefs.

Now, with that mini-synopsis of the Universal Laws, you must become consciously aware and proactive in your thinking. Because what you say, do, and think can create negative thoughts like greed, jealousy, and envy, all fall under the heading of societal dis-eases.

If these dis-eases are not curtailed, the attention they crave, plus the energy required to keep them afloat, will drain you. Ultimately, this negativity will reconfigure and manifest in physical forms.

Case in point, if you have ever known people who interact in negative environments, they will sooner or later pull the toxicity onto themselves.

Therefore, anyone you come into direct contact with that is presenting negativity; you can easily become contagious. *("If you lay down with the dogs, you will get up with the fleas.")* Negativity not only interferes with a consciously aware person thinking deliberate positive thoughts, but it also causes them to become confused.

What is the best way to rid yourself of deleterious thoughts? Simply do not talk about or entertain them in your mind. Instead, do something to feel good, listen to music, dance, hike, walk, bike, but do not focus on lack, limitations, inadequacies, sickness, illness, or unworthiness, etc.

Even positive thoughts can become contaminated if you are always flirting with negativity.

Negativity is a beast; it can cause emotional and physical

collapse inside the human body, embedding itself, causing stress, anxiety, and depression. Stress is one of the most important causes of dis-ease in humans. Whether that stress is physically, mentally, or emotionally induced, it has caustic and long-lasting effects. There are several varieties of stress, good and bad, and everyone deals with it in different ways.

On an average day, most people are coping with some form of stress, and some of that **"Strangling discomfort"** that comes from family members, friends, and work. Or even a perceived happy environment in which the person finds themselves consistently. Positive Thought plays a significant roll in creating your reality; just remember, where you give your attention, your energy flows.

METAPHOR:

Ergo when Jesus came upon the lame Peasant, he did not speak to him about his twisted bones and limp. He addressed only the Destructive Thoughts the Peasant was thinking and exclaimed: "You do this to get the love and the attention you crave." Jesus did not focus on the dis-ease amidst the Peasant as something that could not be healed. Jesus knew that if the seeker just changed his negative and ineffective thinking, he could become whole. Jesus was not trying to correct the physical disabilities, only the physiological ones streaming from the Peasant's deficient Thoughts.

A spiritual intervention? No, a simple message, realign with the Universe through affirmations, meditation, beliefs, deliberate thoughts, and turn your negative thoughts into advantageous ones. Calibrate, eventually, you will be able to change your consciousness to the point it will transform your spiritual and physical body.

IF YOU DON'T
SEEK YOUR
TRUTH...
SOMEONE
WILL GIVE YOU
THEIRS

Chapter 5

Is There a Secret?

Is there a secret? The secret is right there in your mind, and it is called the Law of Attraction. If you can think of your thoughts as oil paints, you can start deliberately imprinting your positive intentions on the canvas of your world. The more you imprint onto your canvas, your dreams, desires, or goals with specific positive thoughts, the richer and more vibrant the object becomes. By practicing the tenets of the Law, you will begin to realign your thoughts in positive ones, knowing you are now able to create your destiny. You must be able to believe the magic starts with the reprogramming of your mind, through Affirmations and Visualization.

Remember Visualization is viewing and feeling yourself already with your desire in your mind. Affirmations are mantras or repeated prayers to enforce your thoughts. There are no boundaries to the comprehensiveness of the energy of creative thought. Just as there is no limit to the mastery of the of the omnipotent infinite mind, your decisive ideas are what creates your experiences and can be an active factor in determining that which you want to be, see and do. The more you use *Decisive, Deliberate Thought* consistently for positivity, and to brand yourself the more you will be able to use it effectively. Whilst, whatever you put behind "**I AM**" you become.

Use these "Act As If"… **"I AM"** affirmative decisive statements with feeling:

- *I am great*
- *I am abundant*
- *I am prosperous*
- *I am confident*
- *I am healthy*
- *I am generous*
- *I am loving*
- *I am joyous*
- *I am excited*
- *I am feeling good*
- *I am aware*

You must be able to believe the magic starts with the reprogramming of your mind. Start immediately reprogramming your conscious and subconscious mind. Through visualizations, affirmations, and mantras, you will instantaneously through repetition spark confidence by doing these exercises daily.

First, if someone asks, *"How are you?"* or *"Are you okay?"* during the day, use **"I Am."** Respond "I Am" doing great, "I Am" wonderful, and "I Am" going to...etc. In essence, when you speak, "I Am," it signals to self and externally to others that you are consciously aware of, and you are decisive. I Am, is also a statement of existence but needs a descriptive tag to make it become a specific thing because it is so infinite. "I Am" is consciousness awareness, infinite in every capacity, and everything you add to "I Am" is add on to you. At the same time, you will also trigger definite manifestation.

Using the phrase **"I Am"** reinforces your self-confidence immensity, by using the power of "I Am," you feel one with your desired outcome, and it is your soul's way of expressing belief in itself confidently. "I Am" is also an anchor in a vortex of chaos and confusion when you're not quite sure of what to say. "I Am" can technically be used in any situation; for example, when you conduct a meeting, you should start with "I Am going to." Use "I Am" as much as possible; "I Am" going to contact you, "I Am going to walk, diet, etc." and feel the magic start.

Can you sense how powerful and decisive "I am" sounds when you say it? The more you use these empowering, uplifting handles, the more you will attract that which you are continually thinking about. *"I Am,"* stated in the positive, changes the ball game. Doesn't that sound great? Great, you say; you talk about being happy all the time, and you haven't been thinking negative thoughts, but nothing is turning outright. Well, one tenet of the Law of Attraction is that words are non-essential. However, your recurring

Thoughts, blended with emotion, create focused energy that reflects how you are feeing. In essence, Thought plus emotion combined with focused energy, causes your inner being to vibrate. This vibration sends a signal out to the Universe, which is akin to the Morse Code, tapping out each desire in short and long messages.

In response to your signal, the Universe complies with the data, the color, size, shape, smell, and the feelings of this desire. In return, it sends you an Earthly physical equivalent of what you are vibrating.

However, if you are talking nonsensically about what you want or wishing for it, these actions will not produce a positive, long-lasting effect on achieving your desire.

An excellent illustration of this omnipotent law is to see yourself as a magnet and to see your friends, family, and business associates also as magnets. The stronger the attraction *(what you desire vehemently)*, the quicker you are drawn toward them, hence a vibrational match.

Because a Thought is energy attracting other similar energies, the Law of Attraction applies to everyone and everything on this planet. The Law responds to your recurring, emotion-filled thoughts the quickest, pulling you towards that which is emitting a similar vibration.

As stated earlier, the Law of Attraction answers to no one and works whether you are negative or positive, aware of its truth or not.

Is this Universal Thought process a coincidence, a blessing, luck, a catastrophe, or *sh*# happening?* Murphy's

Law also says if anything can go wrong, it will and at the wrong time. Most misinformed people use the Law of Attraction in phrases such as *"Birds of a feather flock together; if you lie down with the dog, you will get up with the fleas;* and *be careful of what you wish for because you just might get it."* The Law of Attraction has many phrases; two easy ones to remember are *"What you think about you bring about"* and *"Ask, and you shall receive."*

The best way to experience the Law of Attraction is actually to start asking specifically for what you want and then. Through trial and error, you will learn how to harness the Law's greatness. In a journal, script your story to the point, it resembles a screenplay. Start writing and describing in detail how it feels to be amid your desire. Visualize also that exuberant feeling of being in possession of your desire.

*"As A Man Thinketh He Is-*JamesAllen*"*

If you are looking to find some semblance of spirituality in the Law of Attraction to link your religious beliefs, a very accurate quote from the Bible is, *"As a man thinks in his heart he is."* Specifically, if you think you are healthy, wealthy, successful, worthy, entitled, loving, intelligent, and spiritual, then you shall receive. Equally, the Law's tenets state if you think negative thoughts, similar negative energy will create havoc in your life. A prime example of destructive negativity is holding a grudge against a friend, co-worker, or loved one. The Law of Attraction tenets states that you will attract the same catastrophe you want to happen to another person. It is like drinking poison and expecting the other person to get sick. Negativity manifests and develops itself inside of your body as a dis-ease whose symptoms may include headaches, ulcers, anxiety, and stress, causing extreme discomfort. It would be better to let go of the person and remove him or her physically and mentally from your life, wishing them well. Note that I said "mentally" because even though the person is no longer physically active in your life, you always think about them. You create a mental form of the person and direct your attention and energy towards them. Changing your point of focus, i.e., your conscious awareness to something else will automatically adjust your vibration. **How?** By meditating, walking in a park, bike riding, and observing your environment, that's how you change your point of focus. As you move forward, be proactive and make deliberate choices in developing great, amicable, healthy relationships, in any situation. Then when you make a deliberate choice, it won't be necessary to ask yourself about its consequences. If it's for the *"Highest good of all,"* you can achieve the Universal love, happiness, and desire you strive for in all your endeavors.

Speculate:

1. What is possible?
2. What's stopping you right now?
3. How specific and decisive are you about what you want?
4. Ask yourself: When I have my desire, what will I be sensing, seeing, and feeling that will let me know I actually have it?
5. Ask yourself: Is there any doubt around what I want?
6. Ask yourself: In what way can I begin to "ActAs If"?
7. Ask yourself: Why am I so Confident?

Affirmation: I now know what I want.

INHALE
I AM &
EAT OF THE
UNIVERSE!

CHAPTER 6

The Power of Thought

Imagine being told, when you're first able to walk and talk, that through the power of thought, you would be able to create, design, and control your life. In conjunction with using this universal blueprint, you could become wealthy, healthy, and prosperous. Imagine having the ability to think and focus on specific thoughts and then have what you desire to appear. If you're thinking, wait a minute, this sounds like the television series, Bewitched. Then, you would be right; the same principle applies here: instead of twitching your nose, you need to "think your desires into existence."

Is the **Law of Attraction** enigmatic? Or is this just the greatest secret that the Universe knows, and your soul must rediscover as it reenters into this world?

Can you have what you desire instantly, like in the T.V. series, **"Bewitched"**? Not precisely, because there is something called a Time-warp, where your focused thoughts are suspended for an appropriate amount of time until you to align with your desire mentally and physically. *Why?*

Because if you don't have the space required for the "new," where will you put it? Acquiring the space needed should involve that which is physical, as well as mental. Once the cleaning out of old beliefs, is completed, your manifestation is cued up and waiting in line to come to fruition.

What also stops instant manifestation is the Universe's brilliance of anticipating unprincipled desires. Suppose a person, hypothetically speaking, who is in a fleeting, depressed mental state, had several misguided thoughts about jumping off of a 20-story building. What would stop him?

A time-warp *(a moment of Zen)* a moment of allowing would, an invisible nothingness of space-time suspended between thought and manifestation. This interval would allow the depressed person's time to shift from negative, slightly enough to refocus on the positive aspects of their life. Maybe that's through an aha-moment coming from a flashback of how great their experience has been. This time-warp is the difference between jumping or living life to the fullest.

Therefore, a time-warp is the time in-between the first thought and manifestation used for regrouping, reexamining, and rethinking. To ensure you want to have that experience before the expectancy stage kicks in. For instance, when you are continually looking out your window waiting on UPS or Amazon to deliver a package, this action would increase expectancy. Manifestation is the next phase, invisible and untimely, but it brings to fruition a physical form *(being severed from your order from the menu)*. There still has to be a complete mental engagement to convert thought into the things you are desirously wanting. The time, effort, and willpower must be mental images and visualized in graphic detail to bring forth manifestation.

No matter how hard visualization and **"Acting As If"** may seem stay focused. In your mind, create the mental images of yourself in possession of your desire. Be confident, know you that you have your desire, so repeat **"I Am"** until it comes into fruition. When outside stimuli bombard you, again, stay focused on the outcome you want. Visualize how the puzzle will look once completed, and that should keep you in a state of **Zen-expectation.** This period of expectation is also an excellent time to restructure your mental closets, a check-up from the neck up.

While reorganizing, get rid of those self-imposed, self-induced, outside-influenced, limited negative thoughts born from corrupt beliefs once and for all.

Your Thoughts can decisively change your reality. However, before your thoughts can change your environment, they must change you. How, by thinking with conscious deliberateness. Yes, thoughts can create and change your reality, which is why just because somebody is thinking about something, it will not magically happen. The types of thoughts that can change your reality must be dependable, consistent, and those thoughts must be perceived as if they have already materialized- ergo **"Act As If."**

Thoughts are a mental insight into our ideas, opinions, and beliefs about ourselves and the world around us. While life experiences and education continually form ideas, they are predominantly under conscious control. In plain English, if you are aware of your beliefs and thoughts, you can choose to change them because **Thoughts are things.** They are powerful; the very thoughts running through your mind right now can assist in manifesting the life of your dreams' desires and goals or draw you closer to what you resist—your doubts.

Your thoughts and feelings are energy, including the ones in your subconscious, which are transmitting a precise vibration; out into the Universe. And those vibrations shape the life you are living now. Without a doubt, this is how the Universe operates; in essence, there are particles of energy all around you. These particles coalesce to create your desire. Your thoughts are also energy, the words you speak are energy, and yes, even your actions are energy. You create manifestations through your deliberate, decisive thoughts, words, and actions that use energy to form goals, intent, and experiences.

Now is the perfect time for an extreme consciousness makeover that I spoke of earlier. It would be best if you would seriously indulged in a serious self-analysis, an intense self-evaluation. Because once you know what it is you want, you can easily start manifesting by just thinking in specifics of what you desire rather than being obsessed with what you do not want. Keep in mind what you emphasize in your thinking has a propensity to increase. It is an inescapable and immutable fact that like begets like. To create and attain your goals means you must think decisive, deliberate thoughts every day.

And at least have semblance confidence and believe in yourself.

Most importantly, it would help if you match your beliefs, thoughts, words, to your actions. And straight to the point, **"Act As If,"**- conduct your life as if you already have it, doing it, being it, and then you will be entirely congruent with your thoughts.

Reflect:

1. Are you specific about what you want?
2. Can you Visualize the feeling of having what you want?
3. Acknowledge, nothing limits you but your Thoughts.
4. Ask yourself: How great am I going to feel igniting this passion and action?
5. Ask yourself: What would I do if I knew I could not fail?
6. Ask yourself: How can I make this work?
7. Ask yourself : What amazing and new things will I manifest?

Affirmation: I Feel Great.

IF YOU DRINK
FROM THE CUP
OF UNIVERSAL
KNOWLEDGE,
YOU WILL NEVER
QUENCH YOUR
THIRST

CHAPTER 7

No Limitations

You and only you limit the deliberate creative Thought process inside of your mind that is bursting to get out. Infinite visualization has the power to create your destiny with the help of your imagination. When visualizing, I'm asking you to go into as much detail as you can like a movie a scene, notice the smells, the sounds, what you feel, see and sense yourself with it. While you visualize, allow yourself to be free of any old baggage that you might be saving and holding on. See yourself clear and free of anything negative from your past. It's about making new passionate, enthusiastic, positive choices and freeing yourself from the old non-productive ones.

To activate this creative process of visualization, envision your thoughts as Lego building blocks, adding more detail with each piece. Visualization is like looking through virtual reality goggles and seeing yourself in possession of the object of your desire. So, see yourself already being, doing, having this object your yearning, and say to yourself;

I see myself with it. And This feels good. When is a better time than now to visualize, dream, desire, and

"Act As If".

I know you have heard people make statements like *"Pride goes before the fall,"* or *"It's not your time yet,"* or *"Wait your turn."* I say, wait for what? There is a difference between being confident and knowing what you want and being cocky, arrogant, and conceited. No one will be shortchanged out of their abundance if they attract what they desire. It's your birthright to yearn for, want, aspire because there is an overabundance of wealth, success, and happiness for everyone. First, you must decide you and only you are in total control of your life. That is when you will become consciously aware of what and whom you give your attention.

Would you walk into a shoe store and allow the shoe salesman to tell you which shoes to buy? No, you know what kind of shoes you like and what feels good on your feet.

The moment you realize that you create your reality, start picking superlative words to describe yourself. Immediately start describing yourself as if you are choosing top-grade ingredients to bake a prize-winning cake, pizza, or soufflé because you have the inherent ability to create an unmistakable, irrefutable life deliberately. As you acknowledge this truth, you will never entertain a lack of abundance and limitation on any level in your mind.

Because the moment you start to worry about your

desire *(which is creating the negative)* or use the word **"but,"** it negates everything you want.

Worry slows down and derails your manifestation. The mind cannot focus on the pleasures of your desire and the inner cynical doubts of failure at the same time. Scientists have proven that two energies can not occupy the same space explaining why only one of these energies can dominate your Thought process.

Stop and take responsibility for your positive or negative choices. One must take control of any old beliefs and the voice of doubt to be in a state of receiving abundance. Change your lack of consciousness to one of endless prosperity. Take a deep breath, step back, and give yourself a little time to develop the proper skills to reframe your Thinking process. Because old negative beliefs that you unconsciously previously set into motion will linger and resurface. However, once you get a feel for what you want, start using affirmations and visualization immediately, and Positive Thoughts will start flowing subconsciously. The continuous use of positive affirmations will, at some point, neutralize those old negative Thoughts of lack and limitation, especially the pessimistic, defeatist ones that you have continuously vibrated into the Universe on an unconscious level. Now is an excellent time to start posting pictures throughout your house of your dreams, desires, and goals; this your blueprint to the change you want to happen in your life. Get creative use of your imagination and script an outline about what you want to achieve.

If possible, implement the use of a storyboard or treasure map to be very detailed about your desire. Continually repeat positive affirmations about wealth, abundance, success, and health will slowly dissolve old beliefs of lack and limitations. Look in the mirror and verbalize, feel the emotions connected to the specific details of your desire. Nothing happens in a wishful state of mind. The wish needs to transmute into a yearning with enough emotional energy that would lead to fruition. Focusing on your desire enthusiastically every day will always expedite manifestation. **Yes**, it does take willpower in addition to volition and the determination to bring your desire to fruition. It's the swelling up of your conscious thoughts that ignites the subconscious mind to trigger the spark in your life, like the ignition that gets the car revved up and ready to go.

Now think back to when you were a child, and you heard the bells of the ice cream truck. You knew what kind of ice cream you wanted. You didn't even wonder if the ice cream man had your flavor on the truck; you had faith it would be there. To get the money to purchase the ice cream, you said yes to your parents' demands, regardless of whether there were additional responsibilities you would have performed later. You were off and running after the truck to retrieve your desired treat. This example of how Thought, Desire, Expectation, Volition, and Determination worked together for you back then to bring you sweet, cold, mouth-watering ice cream.

When thoughts become so desirous, the yearning

automatically sets into motion the energy needed for manifestation to come into fruition. In a nutshell, repeated thoughts will start a spark because each time you focus on the same ones, they intensify. The combination of thoughts and emotions automatically creates a passionate yearning. And Thoughts with a clear point of focus will emit enough energy to vibrate vehemently and send a strong signal to the Universe. Thereupon, those similar thoughts are collected, compiled, and then placed an individual file with your name attached. This universal dossier now has the data it needs to decipher your wishes, wants, and desires. Now that the Universe has obtained a sufficient amount of intense thought, passion, emotion, belief, faith, and expectation, it can begin to match the vibrational signal you're sending out. After the Universe calculates this signal, a manifestation is triggered to turn your desire into material form, be it a new car, lover, house, or job.

Do you believe it? Sounds a little simplistic and unconventional. I know this "new age metaphysical dogma" *(what we are, why we exist, and what our purpose is in life)* can change the dynamics of your life or any experiences if you believe you have the will power. Over the past year, I watched people using tablets, MP3 players, and smart-watches on buses, on trains, even at airports, oblivious to anyone or anything around them. Then, it became very apparent to me; people do have the willpower to create their reality if they choose to.

Consciously or unconsciously, most people start

programming their mind the moment they get out of bed in the morning and have that first cup of coffee.

Thoughts are invisible and unobservable, even the ones in your subconscious mind that are already pre-programmed. When you drive off to work, eat lunch, return home, and park the car, have dinner, etc., is there a dilemma? No, because you can proactively program and reprogram your mind to do whatever you want it to do through affirmations, visualization, mantras, and yes, self-hypnosis to make you conscious of all your actions. Whenever possible, while watching TV or listening to music, make sure that what you view or listen to is positive and challenging and something that elevates your consciousness. Inspiring music works cleverly and subliminally on your subconscious mind to induce the reprogramming of your thoughts through repetitive words in songs acting like affirmations. Even your environment takes on a more enthusiastic look because of the energetic vibes you are emitting when singing and dancing around. Believe it or not, you're performing a self-hypnosis technique that allows you to create a lasting positive effect.

Music is Vitamins to the Soul.

Uplifting Motivating Empowering Affirmative

Songs, are a positive mood reviver.

1. I Love Myself
Chaka Khan

2. A Higher Love
Steve Windwood

3. Happy
Pharrell Williams

4. Make It Happen
Mariah Carey

5. I'm Free
The Rolling Stones

6. Get It Right
Aretha Franklin

7. Don't Stop
Fleetwood Mac

8. Nothing's Real But Love
Rebecca Ferguson

9. Think Too Much
Paul Simon

10. If You Want It
Gloria Gaynor

11. Holding On
Disclosure ft. Gregory Porter

12. *(I Am)* **Beautiful**

Christina Aguilera

13. I'm Good

Tim Bowman Jr.

14. Step by Step

Whitney Houston

15. You're Free

Ultra Nate

16. Fly Like An Eagle

Steve Miller

17. You are the Universe

Brand New Heavies ft. Siedah Garrett

18. I Deserve It

Madonna

19. Money On My Mind

Sam Smith

20. Enjoy

Janet Jackson

21. Life!

Jeanne Ricks

22. Follow Your Heart

Tina Moore

23. Ain't No Stopping Us Now

McFadden & Whitehead

24. Free Yourself

Chaka Khan

25. Adventures in Paradise
Minnie Ripperton

26. I Got A New Attitude
Patti LaBelle

27.Keep Your Head To The Sky
Earth, Wind & Fire

28. Smile
Charlie Chaplain

29.Soul Survivor
Beverly Knight

30. This Is It
Kenny Loggins

31. Lohaka
WAH!

32.Pure Imagination
Gene Wilder/Lou Rawls

33. In Time
The Emotions

34. You Can Do It
Linda Clifford

35. Life Is A Song Worth Singing
Johnny Mathis

36. Believe In Yourself
Lena Horne

37.Higher Love
Whitney Houston

38. Unwritten
Natasha Bedingfield
39. Fantasy
Earth Wind & Fire
40. I Am What I Am
Gloria Gaynor
41. Born This Way: I'm On The Right Track
Lady GaGa

After reading the song titles, do you understand now how listening to similar encouraging songs like these can subliminally reprogram your mind? Metaphysically its self-hypnosis wherein your attention is entirely focused on the words of the songs which in some cases give you suggestive positive ideas combined with affirmations at the same time. It is through the repetition of hearing the chorus and familiarity of singing the lyrics that reinforce the desired outcome.

FOR IT IS AT THE
MOMENT, YOU SAY
I AM . . .
IT SHALL BE YOURS

CHAPTER 8

What Do You Want?

How does one find out what they passionately desire? By journaling – writing down all those ideas and wants that you are continually experiencing. And Recognizing the degree of yearning you have for each of them. However, if you don't know what you want, and that's all right, here is a tried and true method to help you find out. First, start by making two lists on a sheet of paper: on one side is for your desires, the other is for things that you **"Don't-Want"** in your life. Under the heading of **"I Want,"** write down things such as a new car, great job, weight loss, a great relationship, healing, etc. Be as specific as you can be to the point of color, shape, size, texture, feel, and when you want it.

Remember the other side is for Don't-Want. Now, looking at the contrast should be an easy task because I always hear people talk about what they don't want.

Start writing down things that are incongruent with what you want to attract, such as a nagging boss, bad relationships, broken down cars, and so forth. Continue to write down anything that you want and don't want, and if you notice a discrepancy between them, do not worry; it's called contrast.

The contrast will be apparent; its the difference between what you want, once you compare the items on the two lists, and what is significant to you. The important stuff will jump out in a specific way; that gives you that aha moment.

How? By highlighting and illustrating what you don't want, you will be able to identify what you do want. This technique will help you firmly figure out your desire and give you some direction and purpose in life. ***Why?*** Because your soul has led you to the point where you stopped and asked yourself what you wanted, to which you replied, *"I don't know."* Many people go through life, never knowing how to achieve their desire. Most aspirants never had to be clear about their desire, and when people asked them what they wanted, their reply usually was, *"I don't want."* Your journey starts when you state what you want positively.

Once you realize how easy it is to produce a plan of action, you will automatically get those vibrational juices flowing freely. You will attract everything and everyone as needed to assist you on your journey. **Your number job is to stay focused!** And to **"Act As If"** your desire has been completed hashtag **#It Is Done.** While on your march. Unfortunately, you may encounter distractions from friends, neighbors, and family. The best way to head off any interference by posting clear-cut pictures of your desire around your house, around your office, and in your car to keep you grounded. These visual reminders will keep your focus and shield you against any unwanted negative thoughts because where you place your attention, your energy flows in that direction. Just envision what you would love to experience during the day. If possible, steer clear of social media distractions like Facebook, Twitter, MySpace, Snapchat, Instagram, Tumblr, etc., unless you are using them for networking purposes.

Now that you have started this quest, you might want to ask yourself, *"Is the desire for you or someone else?"* If the desire is yours, you will be able to move forward confidently. But make sure to love yourself first, regardless of what chaos is going on around you.

If this sounds a little superficial, it's not. Because the vibration of love emotions brings about change faster into your environment because its supercharged with old positive core beliefs, feelings and spiritual radiant energy. Hence the phrase ***"If Momma ain't happy no one in the house is gonna be happy"*** captures how vibrations reverberate silently. Even in silence, everyone knew how Momma felt when she was in a "mood," and not a very good one. Sometimes, words are not necessary to express the feelings that you are experiencing. While your emotions are vibrating and emitting energy and passion into the Universe's Akashic records, which is a repository for all thought.

The ability to create and achieve your desire through

the Law of Attraction is fascinating. And you will want to share your newfound deliberate creating expertise with others. However, you cannot desire for another without their complete participation.

Trying to align with someone else's energy will only leave you entangled in a chaotic vibrational vortex.

A vortex in Metaphysics is a vibrational space said to boost and move your spiritual skills, dreams, desires, and yearnings forward and to help you go to a higher level, And to stretch or expand your consciousness. When you are in alignment with the Universe, you are at peace in your Vortex *(World)* standing in your truth. When you don't align in with the Universe first, then attempt to help another, you will become ***dis-eased,*** and your desire will fall by the wayside and become unattainable due to your lack of focus. *Why?*

Bringing one's desire into manifestation takes a lot of concentrated energy to vibrate and emit a frequency vehemently enough to connect you directly with the Universe. When not spiritually connected to the Universe, the vibrational signal you send out will be weak, causing your desire to be delayed or not fulfilled at all.

Even after knowing this, most people still subconsciously want to use the tenets of the Law Of Attraction to attract desires for others; this is a self-sabotage technique. An obvious distraction from working on their desire, dream, or goal. Sometimes running into a situation you deemed insurmountable or confusing can cause you to take a step back, but you shouldn't let any of that stop you.

What's needed to offset the Self-sabotage effect is a feeling of accomplishment. Even if that means congratulating yourself after you find a parking space. It will be evident that when you are moving towards your desires and goal looking for clarity, there will be detours and setbacks *(there is no failure, only feedback)*. Self-Sabotaging, e.g., procrastination and self-deception, do affect how the Law Of Attraction works, especially during the deliberate creation and the expectation stage. Again, it would be best if you felt super good about yourself as if you had already attracted all your desires and Acted As If. You must feel deserving and push past your comfort zone by proactively wanting and expecting. It is not uncommon to attract something negative, and that indeed will surely test your resolve.

However, it is always better to start with simple attractions and work up yourself to more significant ones that will effectively deliver your desires. At the beginning of working with the tenets of the Law Of Attraction, you will feel a little anxiousness, self-doubt, and even fear of failure. Again there is never failure only feedback for you to tighten up your game.

Don't overthink it or doubt what you want; just move beyond *Negative Thoughts* in your mind. Behind the curtain of self-doubt is the bottom line, which is a **FEAR** of many things one being success. You can conquer fear by having your ideas and actions reflect your desires, dreams, and goals.

Fear is nothing more than not having enough information to sort through the unexpected, unanticipated, or unforeseen. Be proactive and not reactive do your homework research everything you can about your desire. Stop self-sabotaging yourself, procrastinating and hampering your progression look in the mirror with confidence, feeling, decisiveness and say, ***"I can handle the unknown", "I Will", I Am Confident", I Am..., I Am..., I Am...,*** start putting the **"I Am"** before every utterance you say and think. Think about how you went from kindergarten to college, started paying a mortgage, and you are still here.

Cogitate:

1. Declare what you want in the positive.
2. Start using only superlative words to describe yourself.
3. Ask yourself: What will this desire or goal do for me?
4. Ask yourself: Is what I Am doing working?
5. Ask yourself: Am I connected to the Universe?
6. Ask yourself: What can I do to strengthen my confidence?
7. Ask yourself: What Do I Want?

Affirmation: I Am worthy of all that I desire.

POWER HAPPENS
WHEN YOU AGREE
TO ITS POWER

Chapter 9

Making the Connection

You ask, *"What does feeling good have to do with achieving your desire?"* You have to free your thinking from all limitations you have imposed on yourself. The clearer your thoughts are, and the more intense your feelings about your desire are, the stronger the vibrational energy emitted from you is. Those powerful vibrations connect you directly to the universe and then recreate those deliberate thoughts into manifestation. To receive your desire, it is pertinent that you develop your positive aim orient ideas to the point where they can lead to overriding the negative thoughts.

The positive ones will retain more of your attention, and the negative energy will become weak and dissipate. Everything in the Universe and on Earth is made of energy. In humans, energy is both electrical impulses and signals. The vibrations we emit originate from a combination of our Thoughts, Emotions, Soul, Body, and Mind and are made up of universal energy. The formula for Universal energy in motion KE $=. 5 \times m \times v2$. Imagine a two-prong tuning fork; when you strike it against an object, it vibrates and resonates at different frequencies. Depending on how you feel on any given day, your vibrations can be high or low. The more enthusiastic you feel, the more intensive your energy. This leads to a higher vibration, which will attract the object of desire. It's the same kind of dynamic energy you emit when you are in love. Or when you get super excited about purchasing the house or car of your dreams.

On the other hand, if you are feeling quite anguished, the weaker the vibration will be and the lower the output; this creates an inconsistent energy signal. A good example would be when someone is ill, confused, or disorganized, and their body, mind, and spirit are not in sync.

How do you know when you are connecting to the Universe? Once you learn how to meditate and visualize, you immediately will be aware when you are connected or not. First, you will recognize the feeling of being connected when you receive a exuberant uplifting feeling that you are vibrating enough focused energy with positive intent. You will actually feel the difference; a wave of euphoria will encompass you. Think about the last time you were having a conversation on your cell phone, and the call dropped. It appears that you were between cellular towers, and your signal was interrupted due to a transmitting void between your phone and the tower's signal.

Metaphysically speaking once you were reconnected back in sync with one of the cellular towers, the conversation continued. And those dropped calls were the equivalent of being sick, thinking negative thoughts, or not being aligned with your soul. Sometimes, a dropped call is your subconscious mind remembering an earlier negative experience and then disconnecting, not wanting to have the same outcome. However, different experiences *(hate, love, angry, happiness, stress)* create different spiritual connections that bring about mixed emotions. Depending on which feelings get over stimulated, focused signals become more robust and more effective, while others may become weaker and dissipate.

In connecting to the Universe, you must be aware of your feelings and your intentions. It all boils down to what you are thinking and what you are feeling; nothing more and nothing less. That is the first step to becoming proactive, making better decisions, and attracting new, desirous experiences. Yes, here's another excellent example of how the Universal Law of Attraction works. When you feel good, it means you are connected directly to the Universal stream of powerful positive energy. You are not in sync with the Universe, its because you are feeling sad or stressed; hence, a dropped signal and a connection lost. It would be best if you stayed aligned with feeling good, the more enthusiastic, the better.

Connection with the Universe is not as hard as you may think. In reality, you are already connected. It is positive self-realization to want to expand your conscious awareness and connect with the Universe. Everyone has within them a gateway to the infinite intelligence that they can automatically connect to when they reach a specific measure of consciousness development. The Universe is neutral; our connection to it is via the emotions of our feelings, thoughts, and the energy which animates our bodies. All you need to do is to learn how to Meditate, first by withdrawing your attention from your thoughts *(words, ideas, images, memories, fantasies)* and focus your newly freed attention on the overall sensation of the whole physical body.

Now you *(your awareness)* are directly connected to the Universe via the real mental world of energy.

Its believing in the process of Meditating, Visualizing, using Affirmations and having Faith to receive your desire. We invite into our lives what we think about and what we give our attention, whether passionately or fleetingly. And how many of us are carrying around old baggage due to unconscious thinking? Baggage that keeps growing and becoming more significant because we want to prove to ourselves that we were right about our choices, core beliefs, and assessment of life.

"Insanity is doing the same thing over and over and expecting a different result"—
Albert Einstein.

Ponder:

1. Are you sending out clear decisive Thoughts to the Universe?
2. How decisive are you about your desire?
3. Do you understand there is no failure only Feedback?
4. Ask yourself: Do I doubt my abilities to manifest?
5. Ask yourself: What specifically do I want?
6. Ask yourself: What am I going to do to realize my desire?
7. Ask yourself: Why am I so grateful?

Affirmation: Today is the day there is nothing stopping me.

IF YOU COULD TASTE
THE UNIVERSE, YOU
WOULD KNOW IT IS
REPLETE

CHAPTER 10

Collecting Data-Manifestation

Universal laws are always working with us during the day, and it is how we choose to react to them that gives them life. It does not matter to the Universe if you don't believe in the power of the Law ofAttraction or if you don't practice its tenets, but during an average day, most people walk around seeing and sensing things they might like to experience or own. Inevitably, you start thinking about how you can obtain it. *How?*

Everything that you spend more than a moment contemplating is stored automatically in your subconscious mind. Once you become clear about the experience you want to have, from size, shape, texture, and smell, your emotions will kick in to trigger the manifestation action. Proceeding that action is the collection of recurring desirous thoughts, that automatically soak into your subconscious mind and marinate, virtually absorbing all the desires' essence through your six senses. As the thoughts of having the object of your desire exceed your mental enjoyment, the yearning to physically experience it builds to an expectation boil. The clearer those visualized thoughts develop in your mind about how you plan to experience the desire, the faster it will lead to manifestation faster, which includes keeping a strong visual image of your desire sketched in your mind. When enough similar thoughts of the desired experience have collected in the subconscious mind, a signal will vibrate vehemently into the Universe, beckoning manifestation of an earthly physical equivalent. Hence, the Universe acts as a spiritual 3-D manifestation printer bringing your desire to fruition.

How do you get there as fast as possible and in the most time-efficient way? The conscious mind is always taking in almost everything visually before it starts sorting, sensing, analyzing the content. Then it decides which one of your wishes will become one of your experiences based on how much-focused attention you are vehemently spending on the object. As your conscious mind scopes out a new adventure, the subconscious mind, vibrationally, will feel the emotional energy wrapped around the information it is receiving. Emotion is the necessary ingredient to flush out whether you are in a wishful stage or a bonafide desire that you really would like to experience in the future or right now. However, even if it is wishful wishing, the moment you insert enough emotion behind it, you will start the trigger of manifestation.

Again to bring a desire to fruition, you must stay focused on positive, uplifting, empowering Thoughts about your situation. Do not allow others to reroute your desire or become disorganized, chaotic, or confused by external stimulation *(family, friends, spouse, lover, etc.)*. And These are among primary distractions most people contend with on an everyday basis.

However, social media can be a more significant distraction if used for other than networking purposes. If not controlled, you can quickly get sidetracked by distractions which come from all sorts of venues, and can even come from subliminal information. Something that might not be oblivious to many is when watching television and listening to the radio, negativity sometimes is concealed within a commercial message coating. In turn, allowing a person to slowly become hypnotized into believing there is a need for frivolities and engaging in fun things right now. Instead, I say, stay confident and focused on your walk towards your desired or goal and not on neon blinking lights. If necessary, keep quiet about your desire even if it means going into **"the witness protection program"** until it has fully come to fruition; because there are those who mean you well but can not see your vision, and that's ok.

Moreover, knowing that when you can change your *(thinking, ideas, focus)* "Thoughts" and take a different approach to the situation, it may not fall into alignment immediately because the energy and emotion behind the new decision will not be as forceful.

We create our reality through our thoughts, whether by default or deliberate. I want to reiterate how important it is to understand that our thoughts play such an enormous role in our everyday life. Almost every aspect of our lives can be traced back to some notion, feeling idea, thoughts we were thinking about a particular situation. The longer one keeps thinking those same thoughts over and over again, the more they become a reality. Even amid sorrow or greatness, the stronger the attention and emotion are, the more the physical equivalent will manifest. Amazingly your thoughts, being powerful entities, actually does bring the physical form of your desire to fruition. Moving forward in your quest, remember to stop listening and asking for advice from others who you think they have your best interest at heart. These people don't understand the Law of Attraction, and their interpretation can leave you confused and bewildered. Most spiritually unenlightened people may have a strong dogmatic religious bias and try to convince you that success is out of reach and that wanting an abundant, prosperous life is "evil." The less informed will say that successful people are born rich, are lottery winners, or have the right connections, and you must wait for your reward in Heaven.

Hogwash!

When it comes to the bottom line on prosperity, abundance, wealth, excellent health, and opulence and who shall have it, anyone can if they **"Think it into Existence."** And at the end of the day, no one can live your glorious, illustrious, magnificent life now, but you. And, when you have a better understanding of the Law of Attraction, you will know there aren't any restrictions on what you can **"Think into Existence"** with your thoughts when you **"Act As If."** On who may receive wealth, health, and happiness, anyone who visualizes, meditate, and think deliberate thoughts about how they want to see their life now.

Even the Law of Abundance means "there is always enough." When collecting data for your desire, dream, or goal, it is possible to choose the best part of of a model- *(someone that you admire and respect, that fascinates you)*, then *take what you need and leave the rest*. In collecting the necessary data, always "consider the source of information." Don't grab and run; do your research understand why you would need or want to use this information. Investigate as much data necessary for you to be able to **"Act As If"** so, you can to transform your deficient thoughts into a desire. Once you have gathered the information when "Acting as If," stay focused and, in character, feel the feeling of and envision enjoying your new car, house, or networking until you have it perfected. Revel in knowing that your subconscious mind can go beyond the physical and manifest anything you can desirously create in your conscious mind. Nothing is impossible if you think it, have faith and desire it with the most profound passion, and absolutely believe it can be so.

Just remember, it's not your words that create the manifestation, it's non-verbal; it's the feeling you get when you are visualizing, chanting, silently praying, and meditating that triggers the movement to begin fruition.

Muse:

1. Acknowledge that you create your reality.
2. Ask yourself: Am I willing to give of all doubt and fear?
3. Ask yourself: How determined am I?
4. Ask yourself: Am I definite, and decisive enough about my desire?
5. Ask yourself: When will I start Thinking It Into Existence?
6. Ask yourself: Do I have the faith and belief I can achieve my goal?

Affirmation: I am worthy of my desire.

IF YOU OPEN YOUR
EYES, YOU WILL
KNOW IT'S OK TO
LET YOUR MIND OUT

CHAPTER 11

Acting As If

What is the "Act As If" principle? Is it *"Fake it till you make it"* or make-belief, pretending play-acting, or just a placebo effect? Believe it or not, it is behavioral psychology, an approach to changing your thought process to motivate you by modeling success. The 1880's philosopher, William James, said, "As If" declared that if you change your behavior and your dysfunctional thoughts, you, in turn, will change. When your emotions are involved, you change your behavior. Actually, by paying attention to your idiosyncrasies, you will begin to transform your behavior.

Try sitting in a power position for a while; you will immediately start to feel more confident. Smile when you are feeling exhausted, and you will automatically start feeling better. Does this sound a little pollyannaish? Research has proven the validity of these exercises. "Act As If" is designed to help people change their ineffective behavior and begin to build confidence. To "Act As If" is to mentally recreate your life by putting yourself physically into the situation.

Or a person persona; thus, mimicking their style. Think, talk, dress, use facial mannerisms, and posture until you feel as if you are adopting their internal drive to succeed. To "Act As If" is to become consciously aware of everything around you. To "Act As If" is taking proactive affirmative action to transform your life by eliminating procrastination and having faith in your ability to deliberately create the experience you now want to live. Use the "Act As If" technique to help ignite your desire. Suppose your desire is to own a restaurant, then "Act As If" the kitchen in your house is already set up as a gourmet-quality restaurant

When approaching the "**Act As If**" technique above all, you must believe and have faith in yourself, and nothing else will matter. It's the first initial step in becoming confident. However, if you want to become confident in using metaphysical, spiritual laws, it is necessary to become a person who exudes mastery in his or her field. Practice repeatedly in front of a mirror or with loving friends until the feeling of being confident overtakes you. Is this "fake it until you make it" a phenomenon? Perhaps, but that's a reckless way to proceed once you understand the dynamics of "Act As If," which goes past the superficiality of just mimicking someone. The *"fake it until you make it"* technique to instant success requires no techniques; its a monkey see monkey do, which is quite suspicious. To "Act As If" you have to retrain, redress, and reprogram your powerful core beliefs driven mind; in addition, you will need to put into practice the Universal Laws.

Once you realize that there is a new way of using the power of your thoughts, you can change your consciousness. ***How?*** You can do this by using one of the most impressive sci-fi gadgets, Virtual Reality goggles. Virtual *(simulated)* and reality refer to the experiences we humans have every day. However, instead of using a head-mounted device for immersing a person in a digital 3D environment, it is achieved by using your imagination.

To **"ActAs If"** lets you have an experience a preconceived reality with the intent to interact in a seemingly real or physical way. Virtual Reality, which is visualization, uses your imagination to produce the illusion of reality, enables you to immerse yourself in your desire without constraints. Once you deliberately think about and know what you want and believe you can have it, you will finally be able to attract your desire. Start pretending right now; "Act As If." "Think It Into Existence" as anything in the world your heart desires, and then "ActAs If" ASAP.

If, at this point in your life, you are not successful or unhappy, take a new proactive look in life. I'm suggesting that you consider another way of thinking that will cost nothing. The first step toward that desire or goal would be to ask yourself, "How can I make my situation better?" Furthermore, is your old way of thinking working in your best interests? Are you achieving anything? If not, then using a little non-magic, magic-like 'Acting As If,' it might help. You must also be mindful though of using all the resources that you have on hand to move forward. One excellent resource is your feelings, and the other is the recurring thoughts about wanting to change your life. The thoughts that you visualize in your mind will materialize, and as you "Act As If" you can create your unique reality.

If you aspire to a profession where business-casual attire is required, make sure you dress and act the part. It would be best if you reached for compatible with your Model and also find a way to fit into their culture and environment as much as possible. Make sure to fit in authentically as possible and be consciously aware, or else your pretending could become disastrous. Do your research so that you become bonafide and do not stick out like a sore thumb. Yes, Model your sponsor, but not to the point it is evident that you are mimicking them to any outside observer. "Act As If" with a clear focus intent.

Next, insert powerful descriptive thoughts into your visualization, add all the sensations of the way something feels, smells, and taste, to the point that you can reach out and touch the experience. Immerse yourself to the point that you can feel every sensation. What are you aware of now?

Seriously, "Acting as if" cost you nothing. There is barely any energy expended except to recreate the physical motions necessary to complete the task. Acting in a certain way will allow your brain to rehearse and adapted the thoughts you need to accomplish the task. Incorporate the **"Act As If"** technique into every aspect of your daily routine, i.e., *"I am always on time," "I always eat the right food."* *I Am great, I Am prosperous, I Am…*

Again, "Act as if" every time you want to fulfill the desire feel the sensation of owning that fantastic new car you've been craving. Pretend to the point that you can smell the new-car aroma.

You must remain diligent, even in the light of when others think you are acting a little weird or eccentric. Just remember to stay focused and do not deter from "Acting As If." How you perceive yourself reflects in the way you walk, talk, and look, it is your body language, which is what will be seen and reflected to those you wish to impress. And the specific people who you want to attract will recognize your mission as you "Act As If." When you have to act, envision unlimited abundance, and create what you want to experience at any given moment in time.

The Laws of the Universe are the blueprint to deliberately creating a new experience. If that is what you are seeking, your imagination and visualization will supply the tools necessary to get you there. You are pre-designing your reality in the future through positive or negative thoughts, whether you think it's possible or not. It would be easy to say if you don't like something, then don't think about it or don't think negative thoughts; however, **"What you resist persists."** If you have a feeling, you are going to encounter an uncomfortable situation and go the offensive expending precious energy or be exemplary and offer the first smile to reduces stress. Then, at the start of the conversation, affirm your intention, and immediately start sending out powerful, enthusiastic, positive, constructive thoughts. Watch how the changing of the energy from negative to positive, gets your desired outcome, and it should coincide perfectly.

A proactive adage…

"Think before you speak."

The Law of Attraction is not capable of distinguishing between a negative or positive experience. The Universe responds to the vibration of the sensation you desire. The Law of Attraction says here's more of that sensation you're experiencing, whether negative or positive. It can be said; You've made your bed, now lay in it!

Reframe your thoughts instead of concentrating on unwanted objects or passionately expressing, *'I don't want this* or *I don't like that,'* which uses up a lot of positive energy. State what you want in the positive. Begin with what you desire, for example, and *I want to experience this, I would like that,* i.e., a car, a house, clothing, electronics, etc. Especially speak about what you desire in the positive. State your preference also in the affirmative and 'Act As If' you already have it in your possession. Once you begin to desire it, embrace the sensation and think about it, to the point that you can smell it, feel it, and taste it.

Then set your mind and body into motion and 'Act As If,' till you believe you already have it in your grasp. If this means reading a script, to capture the essence of the character of the person, then do it. Continue, even if it feels a little artificial or forced, and you will get into the swing of it, in time. Intuitive knowledge comes with feeling confident, and that will outweigh any uncomfortable feelings.

Start imagining that you have your desired career, etc., feel the sensation and immerse yourself into the vision. Concentrate specifically on the experience and give it enough emotional energy, so that the Universe vibrates and sends you this object. Then, with confidence, 'Act As If' you already have achieved your desire. However, before this manifestation occurs, you must also begin to interact with similar people who you admire. Go to the places they go to change your physicality and environment mentally.

By going to these places, your Model goes, you get more clues on how to **"Act As If."** Please continue to do this until it becomes a natural part of what you want to embody. The Universe doesn't have a mechanism to detect whether you are pretending or if it's the real deal. Pretend to the point that you think you are confident enough to possess the object of desire. And then and only then will the Universe match it. Once you are mentally aligned with your desire and have physically made room for it in your life, manifestation cannot be denied.

Now, deliberately put the Law of Attraction into practice because *"faith without action is nothing or procrastination"* *(James 2:17)*. Don't delay, start right now, and march toward abundance.

Act the part start pretending. "Act As If"! until it does not feel like your pretending anymore. "Act As If" until you can not physically tell the difference between your ability and your Model. If it's a car you desire again, have the confidence to go to a car dealership, get in sit down in that new car. Sit in your boss's chair, conduct yourself as he would, and feel the power. Stop by a jeweler and try on that diamond ring and feel the opulence as if you already own it. Always remember, the subconscious mind doesn't distinguish between the real world and a virtual one. When "Acting as if" act accordingly, if you want to be rich, act rich. Visualize yourself first as prosperous and then physically step into the scenario by looking the part. Present yourself in the appropriate attire if necessary, purchase the right clothes for your desired profession.

Ideally, you must look the part, but beyond that, you have to feel it and speak about it as if you were already living the experience. That's right **"Think It Into Existence"** "Acting As If" will cost you nothing, nor does it take a great deal of energy. Besides the physiological effects *(breathing, body stance, and facial expressions)*, the body goes through emitting vibrations when "Acting As If," you can effortlessly apply this technique to any subject regardless of the experience or qualifications.

Yes, even when pretending you need to change your mannerism, it's like going to a masquerade party or dressing up for Halloween – you immediately become the character.

So, add all the personality traits you can; you need to become immersed in the new '**you**' and allow others to respond to you as such. Your conscious mind, which is suspicious and cautious, will believe its game and not reject or judge the information you are deliberately creating. And pass it on to the subconscious mind where it will start collecting enough data on the subject to pass on to the Universe for manifestation. Get crystal clear and confident about changing your life and disregard any naysayers' criticisms.

"What Other People Think of You Is None of Your Business" --Eleanor Roosevelt.

Be proactive, **Think it into existence,** design your life just like you design your house, clothing, new car, and yes, even your dinner. Why not commit to "Act As If?"

Believing in yourself is unquestionably the most significant step. You have got to believe in the "**I Am**" of who you are *Thinking Into existence*. Of course, nothing in the Universe happens instantly, but with decisive, deliberate practice, ultimately, "Acting As If" is going to make you feel more confident in manifestation and make your visualizations come to fruition sooner rather than later. Because *"If you believe it, you can achieve it."* If you have the faith of a mustard seed, you can design anything in your life.

Act As If What You Do Makes A Difference. It Does.--William James

Surmise:

1. Start "Acting As If" you have already received your dream, desire or goal.
2. Declare what you desire is already in the now.
3. Ask yourself: Can I visualize and stay focused on what I want?
4. Ask yourself: Do I actually see myself with my desire.
5. Ask yourself: Is this goal realistic?
6. Ask yourself: What prevents me from having this goal right now?
7. Ask yourself: Do I realize how thrilled I Am going to be when my desire comes to fruition?

Affirmation: I am worthy of all that I desire.

YOU CAN HAVE IT
ALL IF YOU REACH
INSIDE & REDIRECT
THE CALL

Chapter 12

Questions, Answers, & Thoughts:

1. Question: How do I stop thinking that I cannot achieve my goal?

Answer: No one and nothing has power over you; only your Thoughts. Your Thoughts create different experiences in your life. If you feel great about the situation you find yourself in, then the Universe will send more of that wonderful feeling. However, if you are not in a place of feeling good, you will receive more of that negative feeling. Why? It has everything to do with your "Point of Focus." Where you focus your attention on good, bad, or indifferent, it will cause you to automatically fixate on the object, bringing more of the same energy streaming towards you. Treasure Mapping, Journaling, and positive affirmations are great "Point of Focus" techniques.

Sometimes it's a little hard to hear that everything is

possible. Together with that, there is no such thing as a failure because failure is just feedback to start anew.

It is mind over matter, which sounds like pop cultural psycho-babble, but it's true. Think, Desire, Visualize, Expect, and Receive it for the **"Highest Good of All."**

2. Question: How will I know if what I desire is right for me?

Answer: This is the second most asked question right behind "What do you want?" When something is right for you, your willingness to do it will be so great that even if you do not get paid for it, it will not bother you. The intense thirst for experiencing this "It" will be so great, that nothing else in life will satisfy it. You will know it is right because the experience makes you unconditionally happy. Beyond that, it is something you want to share with others. Now quench this thirst, embrace your desire, and go for it.

3. Question: Do I have to pretend to be happy and joyful when I am not?

Answer: Yes, because when you 'Act As If,' you will immediately reset your mood. The moment you shift to positive thoughts, you begin to move into a more uplifted state. Then you will immediately start feeling better about your situation. Your thoughts are what put you in total control of your life. The ability to choose how you react and feel helps to create your life; your attitude is everything.

Being happy is a natural state, and it aligns you more quickly with the Universe.

4. Question: Will I have to monitor my thoughts?

Answer: Yes, but not to the point where you try to guard against every negative thought that pops into your head. Being conscious of your thoughts is the first step to being proactive about your life. Taking charge of your thoughts and making discerning choices help you speak specifically about what you want to manifest.

5. Question: How specific must I be when I am thinking about my desire?

Answer: The more specific you are, the greater the chance of receiving your desire resembling your vision. "Act As If" gives full details of your desire. Start by using all of your senses: sight, sound, taste, and touch. See yourself interacting with the situation --embrace it, expect it, and believe it is yours.

Example: I want a large vacation home on a secluded Caribbean Island on a hill. I want floor to ceiling windows with a view of the ocean and the mountains. I want hard bamboo flooring throughout the house to make it easier to sweep up the sand after coming from sitting on the beach. I want the kitchen to have a stainless steel double oven. So, when I am cooking, I can bake hot chocolate chip cookies and roast hazelnuts with a touch of cinnamon at the same time. I see myself entertaining my friends and family by the pool as we dance under the moonlight.

6. Question: Do I have to quit my job to pursue my desire?

Answer: No, use your current position as a launching pad. Do you know what makes the business where you currently work successful? If not, learn all you can. When you feel strongly enough about your desire and are spiritually connected, slowly remove yourself from your job, or continue to work there until it becomes a part-time situation. Any data you can collect is only going to be helpful as you vehemently visualize your desire.

7. Question: Is a journal a good use to write down my thoughts?

Answer: It is an excellent idea. A simple notebook is a great place to start writing specifics about your desires, using the pages to document your progress from day to day. Use effective milestones to monitor your attraction progress.

Example: A prime example of a great use of a journal is to retake another look at question #5. But beyond writing, incorporate a calendar with appointments and networking gatherings that you need to attend inside of the journal.

8. Question: Is there an easier way to accomplish dreams, desires, and goals, and what would be those steps?

Answer: *First, ask yourself the following questions:*

*   What do I honestly want?
*   Why do I want to attract this situation, object or desire?
*   What stops you right now from having this dream, desire or goal?
*   What old beliefs are holding me stuck?
*   What resources do I have on hand now that I can use for my benefit?
*   What is my genuine commitment to seeing my desire to completion?
*   Do I mentally see myself successful, healthy, wealthy and abundant?
*   Is my attitude positive and am I grateful for what I have now?
*   What specific actions will I take towards my desire?
*   What will motivate me to go on full ?
*   What incentive will I use for myself to get you to the goal?
*   When am I expecting my manifestation?

9. Question: How long does it take to master the Law of Attraction?

Answer: It is not the mastering of the Law that makes it work, it is the acknowledgment that it is working all the time, and all you have to do is tap into the flow. It's about becoming proactive and always using "I Am." The moment you start speaking "I Am," reprogramming of your conscious and subconscious mind begins. It is about soaking up every "I am" and turning it into reality.

10. Question: Is the Law of Attraction taught in church?

Answer: Some churches, religious and spiritual centers, do teach the Universal Laws. Be astute and pay attention to how certain metaphysical and religious phrases have the same meaning, but are translated differently.

Example:

Lord: Which is also considered to be a derivative of the word **Law.**

As a man thinketh in his heart, so he is. *Proverbs 23:7.*

As a Man Thinketh: A metaphysical book, by James Allen.

Cause and Effect: Everything you do negatively or positively will surely come back to you.

Whatsoever a man soweth, that shall he also reap. *Galatians 6:7-9.*

Do unto others as you would have them do unto you. *Luke 6:31.*

Karma: Justice is determining a person's state of life based on past life actions or deeds; a Buddhism principle.

Do not be deceived: Bad company ruins good morals. *Corinthians 15:33.*

Birds of a feather flock together: Be careful of those you choose to associate with because you may become like them.

11. Question: Is this Universal Law of Karma Cause & Effect?

Answer: Not really, but similar. The Law of Attraction is, "What you think about, you bring about." The Law of Cause & Effect is like a domino effect; one action will lead to a series of events; basically "You reap what you sow." Karma, on the other hand, deals with deeds and actions from a previous life, in conjunction with your actions and reactions today. "Do unto others as you wish to have done unto you."

12. Question: How can I develop an attitude of Gratitude when my life is shaky?

Answer: When you wake up every morning, and you are physically and mentally intact, give thanks.

Begin with "I am" grateful for…Be thankful for what you have in your life "now." An attitude of Gratitude also starts with showing appreciation for your home, your spouse, your lover, your dog, cat, car, relations, and friends. The love or warm feelings that you receive from others is a reflection of what you have given, and it shows that they are grateful. When you look at your environment, it is apparent that you are probably in a better situation than most, so show some kindness. Also, be grateful that you can read the typing on this page.

13. Question: How does prayer figure into this process?

Answer: Prayer is a magnificent tool to connect you directly to the Universe. Abasic prayer is usually a request or an imploration for something that is wanted. However, when implementing the Law of Attraction, if you are specific when asking for a blessing (divine intervention), the Universe will reply, "Give that person more of what they are desiring and asking for." When praying, imploring, or meditating, do it from a place of gratitude, not from lack. Pray, but don't beg; be vigilant. Once you state what you desire, stay passionately focused, but do not try to figure out the outcome; let the Universe take it from there.

14. Question: Can I use this Law to overcome an existing medical condition?

Answer: Always consult with a medical professional before you decide to use an alternative method. However, when you think positive, healthy thoughts about any situation, you change the dynamics.

15. Question: What's the most important point that I should take from this book?

Answer: When "Acting As If," The Law of Attraction becomes proactive versus reactive.

The use of Law of Attraction tenets is branding you with **"IAM."**

When you use The Law of Attraction, it will help you hold mental influence over your environment. Basically, it is sending out thought waves to attract and affect those who would conspire with you to bring about your desire.

Affirmation: I am healthy, wealthy, prosperous and abundant.

I AM
THAT WHAT I THINK
I AM

An IDEA With
FEELING… Is A Fire
With Inexhaustible Fuel!

CHAPTER 13

When can I start?

The Law of Attraction with it limitless infinite possibilities is always working, with or without your consent. Yes, you can start *"NOW."* These Exercises can be applied in the real world, just by adjusting your consciousness to accept a new way of thinking. The Law of Attraction never stops delivering on your desires, especially the ones tucked neatly away in your subconscious mind. Even desires you've yearned for and wondered why they have not materialized. Nevertheless, no invitation or RSVP is needed for the Law to work directly for you. Learn the steps **1.)** Have desirous specific thoughts. **2.)** Desire the experience vehemently. **3.)** Visualize and feel the sensation. **4.)** Believe in the possibility of self-manifestation. **5.)** Act As If.

One of the biggest stumbling blocks you will face moving forward is your **Core beliefs.** Those stubborn Core beliefs are the foundation of all your beliefs—the ones you have acquired from your parents, teachers, and the environment. As a result, some of these beliefs are cultural and carried from childhood into adulthood. However, some are just old wives' tales you would swear were even ordained, but they are not. Core beliefs limit your experiences to infinite new ideas. To change, self-limitation you must do a self-evaluation and remove unnecessary clutter from your mind. Start now: delve right in and get rid of your old crippling beliefs, particularly beliefs and habits that are not consistent with what you desire and where you want to go.

Stay focused on what you want to accomplish. In order to be proficient in attracting your desire and experience, you must take a big leap of faith. Unquestionably, having blind faith is a big pill to swallow, but applying the tenets of the Law of Attraction can be done. Everything you do from this day forward must coincide with moving towards accomplishing your desire. Start with opening your mind to new ideas and creative thought processes. You trust that the sun will rise tomorrow, and the earth will revolve around the sun, without doubt; that is faith.

When people are not aware of the metaphysical concept of the Law of Attraction, it's easy to say it doesn't work. Instead of learning to create and allowing the process to work, people let doubt slip in, corrupting their thought process. There are independent scientific data that supports how the Law of Attraction's principles work. The Law of Attraction is based on a metaphysical theory dealing with converting thoughts into energy and physical form and has been documented since 1877.

If you want to apply the science of the Law of Attraction, you need to be decisive and establish that you want to change your life. That includes leaving behind core beliefs such as I'm not good enough; I'm not worthy; they won't let me because I'm too short/ tall; my mother/father, etc., told me it was wrong; I don't have enough experience, and of course, I have to wait my turn or time. Sound familiar?

Don't let these negative core beliefs stop you. Your experiences are only fettered to you by what you think it can be for you. Most of core beliefs are excuses or lies you tell yourself, friends, and family, to justify your failure to not take responsibility for your non-action. Stop making excuses; admit that fear and failure exist to remind you to regroup, rethink, and refocus on your needs/wants. Naturally, you want to move forward, and that takes work, mental and physical.

Form a crystal-clear, mental picture of where you are now and where you want to go: now, it's time for the reprogramming to start. Moving forward consists of **asking** pertinent questions of **yourself,** like the following:`

* **What stops me from getting what I want?**
* **What additional resources do I need?**
* **Am I visualizing with specificity?**
* **Am I feeling the essence of what I want?**

* Am I being truthful and honest with myself about wanting this Desire?

These self-examination questions will help you think specific, precise, focused Thoughts. Use these exercises for recall, as well as to see where you are right now on your path. Let your journal be a document to review. Where you were in your past and what you want to accomplish in the future, write it down. Meditate, and while you visualize, allow yourself to be free of any old baggage that you might be holding onto intensely. See yourself clear and free of anything from your past.

Use a journal to record your thoughts about your desires. Write down any old childhood beliefs and compare them with your new ones. Are these ideas still relevant now? Every thought is the start of a unique experience that can be capitalized on to create deliberately. The journal can become your blueprint for success and the place to document your progress during the day. And simultaneously, for the act of checking, adjusting by comparison your now feelings with your soul's higher paradigm, basically fine-tuning your desire while in a calibration session in an exact and precise way.

In all actuality, you will be able to calibrate; to plan your intention deliberately, so you will know precisely why you want it. With this information, it will be like saying you already made it! Because whatever has happened, you've done it, and that's in the past. With new awareness comes new knowledge. In as much, you will also be able to document that you forgive yourself and others for whatever you perceived as unfavorable that happen to you. You are living in the "Now" and consciously aware of how to deliberately create; by making decisive choices attracting everything you want.

Cogitate:

1. ActAs If, now!
2. Set yourself free of any mental limitations.
3. Are your Thoughts positive and constructive?
4. Ask yourself:Am I entertaining Thoughts of lack and limitation?
5. Ask yourself:Are your Thoughts about abundance?
6. Ask yourself:Am I grateful for what I have experienced?
7. Ask yourself: In what ways can I achieve my goals?

Affirmation: There is no limitations in my life.

Inside My
Mind…
I can Create
Worlds of
Magnificence

CHAPTER 14

"Act As If" Review

1. Decide what you want... does it fit into your life?

2. State what you desire in the positive with enough emotion to make it feel physically real.

3. Think repeatedly during the day about your desire and visualize it.

4. Realign your thinking, using your willpower to get started and then allow your feelings to help you set your goals.

5. Mentally and physically sync with whatever you, Desire to the point of manifestation.

6. Understand all possibilities are limited by the Thoughts in your mind.

7. Start pretending, a/k/a "Acting As If" until you feel Confident enough to thrive on your own.

8. Be specific: include the size, shape, color, texture, smell and when you want your desire.

9. Use affirmations and empowering songs to change old beliefs until the new, positive ones become a habit.

10. If you don't want the situation or experience, do not give your attention to it, or change your point of focus.

11. Please post pictures of your dreams, desires, and goals everywhere and visualize having them.

12. Believe, have faith, be confident, speak in the positive, and take personal responsibility.

13. Keep a journal; write specific details about your desire and feel the sensations.

14. Model someone who has the positive traits you desire, and use common sense.

15. Stay focused and on point, be aware. Read, review, reprogram.

16. Start small, gain confidence in creating and manifesting.

17. Become proactive, consciously be mindful of yourself and your surroundings.

18. Believe and expect that it will be yours, that includes wealth, health, success, and abundance.

19. Acknowledge that you are a mental magnet and will attract to you everything you are thinking and feeling.

20. Be aware and be willing to change your environment.

IF YOU DON'T KNOW
WHAT YOU WANT ...
SOMEONE ELSE WILL
DECIDE FOR YOU

Chapter 15

Think it into Existence

In my search to find excellence, people have often told me that in most self-help books, ***"They didn't tell me how to apply it."*** I say, don't be deterred; be determined to change your life. The power to create your reality is straightforward "Think It Into Existence." Again, how simple is that? But before you contemplate what you want, you must take time to **"Zen."**

What is Zen? Its a state of consciousness, a real state of focus that incorporates a total cohesiveness of body and mind. Basically, it means to Chill and Calibrate to become peaceful, enlighten, introspective and communicate with the Universal power within yourself. Start with meditation, which means relax, rejuvenate, clear the mind of all things and reconnect consciously with the Universe. If you are so inclined, you can do a quick meditate at any time, in your office on the beach on a streetcar or a mountain top it does not matter.

Stop and close your eyes for a minute, be still, silent

and, stop the thoughts in your head as much as possible, and receive the divine.

I call meditation a "spiritual medication" once adapted into your daily routine its truly a whole different world; I say *a **Prayer** is uploading to the **Universe**, and **Mediation** is downloading from the **Universe.*** If used correctly, meditation can spiritually transform you. I know a lot of people who believed that they could never learn to meditate. Meditation is nothing new; it has been around since time began and practiced in some form by most religions.

Once more, here's a formula for meditation for the novice. Allow yourself several minutes or a longer duration of time, but the shorter, the better until you get used to the feeling of being connected to your inner self. First, put on some guided meditation music, set a timer. Sit or layback in a comfortable chair clear your mind of all thoughts, focus your attention on your breathing exhaling and inhaling slowly. If your mind wanders, no problem refocus. Now notice how your body feels all over as your breath moves in and out of your lungs. Simply breathe naturally.

You should feel a feeling of wellbeing come over yourself. Maintain your session as long as possible to get all the positive effects of tranquility and peace of mind.

If practiced daily, meditation can lead to spiritual enlightenment experiences, improved concentration, enhance self-awareness, reduce stress, and reduced social anxiety. Remember, all it takes is a small reasonable amount of time, a scheduled period in your day.

Now, what does your consciousness say about Visualization, Meditation, **"Act As If"** and "I Am"? Are you aware of your thoughts, feelings, and emotions? Do you know what you want now?

Do you understand that positive thinking alone will not change your mindset and that it takes a total mental commitment from you to make a change in your life?

Can you remember a period in your like when you were in at the top of your game? Unbeknownst to you, it was because you were focused, and your attention was laser intense on your desire. If you didn't practice the Law Of Attraction, it was by default. But now that you know how to use the Law and understand that it works, whether you work it, you can start deliberately creating anything your hearts desire.

What if you knowingly took that same focused energy and started mentally projecting those deliberate, focused thoughts into the Universe.

Yes, vibrate- ***"Think it into Existence"*** until you've emitted enough pure positive energy to the point it will put your true intent in total alignment with the Universe.

Virtually without hesitation, grab some of those same energized good feelings and thrust them over into tomorrow. Believe it or not, those projected feelings will be waiting there for you to utilize them throughout the day, which is kind of like paying it forward. As significant as the current moment is, stop and visualize the perfect outcome to make your tomorrow even more spectacular.

The task ahead for you now is to gain control over your thoughts. Calibrate be cognizant; of how you want to feel at any given moment it is a must. Start with positive affirmations, like *"I feel good, I am great,* I got this, and I know everything all ways work out for me and tomorrow is gonna be even more fantastic, and contain more of this. My point is you need peace of mind in your life to make better choices. Even more critical, through visualization and meditation, you can deliberately create your reality.

First, you must awaken yourself from the zombie-like state you've been living, and stand up and take personal responsibility for your life. Practice The Law of Attraction from the moment you awake in the morning, by meditating, visualizing, and saying to yourself; ***I Am that which I think I am.*** Deliberately direct your mind towards your desire and **"Act As If"** it's already accomplished. Verbally say, to yourself, "It is done" and feel the emotion of completion. Decide to be proactive and use your imagination to see yourself with being, doing, touching, and having it, and yes, sense the outcome of your day.

As you become more consciously aware, sit in silence, and calibrate if easier meditate. Introspectively, ask your soul to speak the universal truth you need to hear. Think about what you want to convey to the Universe, and start every day, setting forth these positive intentions before you think another thought or talk on the phone to anyone.

Now that you feel more confident start attracting little desires, and build on to bigger ones. Make sure you remember as you flex your wings and experiment that there is no failure, only feedback.

Undeniably what the mind can conceive and believe the mind can achieve.

Therefore use your Law of Attraction skills and start with something as simple as the parking space to build confidence. Once you feel a sense of accomplishment, use more detailed thoughts to work on a more significant desire. By all means, once you gain confidence, be very specific and clear about what you desire; then, "ActAs If."

Get **M-a-d!** *(Make A Decision)* This laser focused intense feeling of acting will set into motion a universal connection that cannot fail you because once emotional energy starts to vibrate, the Universe doesn't distinguish between what is imaginary or real. Tell me what would you do if you knew you could not fail?

When you understand your thoughts are living things functioning for the sole purpose of creating your desired reality, you will treat them with respect.

Every experience you want to have and can imagine is yours for the asking. The power of your deliberate thoughts puts you in total control of your life. Therefore your focused attention allows you to create anything you can imagine.

Wherefore, if you can think, desire, and believe it, you can achieve it.

Yes, through Visualization with its awe-inspiring power to form mental nonphysical, physical feeling visual images in your mind.

Now fantasize about all the desires you would like to attract and indulge in from this vast array of world experiences.

Ergo, as you march forward, keep in mind your attitude is everything; it plays a vital part in how you feel and react in any given situation. Once you use your will power not to sub come to outside events and people you will be able to alter your attitude to one of being positive, the definite choices you make will dictate when and how you get what you desire.

The Law of Attraction is a phenomenon a Spiritual Law that can create unbelievable situations through the secret power of your thoughts. Once you believe in and adopt the tenets of the Law of Attraction, you automatically become the CEO of your life. It's truly incredible. In combination with an attitude of gratitude, you will create your vision beyond any of your core belief have to lead you to believe. When first applying the Law of Attraction, it will feel like a vortex opened up and said it's OK to feel a little overwhelmed with this mysterious, invisible power.

There have been many great teachers from the past century and today who have known and used this power.

New Thought giants Genevieve Behrend, Thomas

Troward, James Allen, Johnnie Colemon, Ernest Holmes, Wallace D. Wattles, Napoleon Hill, Louise Hayes, and Florence Scovel Shinn were all students at one time. They became enlightened on how to create deliberately.

By all means, stand up and take personal responsibility for your life. Don't allow yourself to be frozen in time or caught standing still, stuck, and afraid to decide; what you'll need to change your life. Because there is no reason for you to be if I may **"Stuck."** There is always a way to get **Unstuck**, sometimes all it takes is for you to pivot.

In essence, to create a new you, one must reach way down into your soul and grab hold of your inner strength and redirect it to your **"I Am-ness"** at the gut level of your feelingness.

But before you can have anything on Earth, you must first see it in your mind and then specifically define yourself, as the person you want to be and then "ActAs If."

Because the subconscious mind learns through repetition and "Act As If" boosts the learning by 1000 times. You must continually define yourself as the one who wishes to be, I Am-. But first, in your mind's eye, use your imagination to create the inspiration and, through visualization, see yourself with it and feel as if you already have it. Essentially, if you want your desire to manifest asap, get crystal clear about your choice, decision, and then write it down, review and rehearse to point you know it inside out.

When a person defines himself as that which he desires to be, they will realize all the wasted time they spent being indecisive; they only needed to see themselves mentally with their goal. In essence, they would have expedited their desire sooner rather than later. And, along the way, recognized there's plenty of abundance for everyone, and no one needs to compete with others freeing themselves from wasting precious energy. It sounds a little existentialism, like in the movie **Wizard of Oz** when Dorthy was ready to go home. First and foremost, all she needed was to remove herself from the unpleasant situation she found herself was to believe in herself, to know her heart, have courage, become decisive, and make a declarative statement, '**I**_____ ''.

Thus knowing what you want and having enough confidence in yourself to now choose deliberately will consistently be like going shopping and buying anything you want.

Unlike Murphy's law, *"what can go wrong will go wrong,"* a negative sentiment to keep you from getting involved or fully taking charge of your life. The Law of Attraction on the other hand only gives you more of what you focus your attention on.

So don't spend your time self-sabotaging or finding fault in others. To get more of what you are vibrating, pure positive energy, you must give your attention to only that which you are seeking. In addition to elevating yourself to be that which you want to be, you must stop all judging and self-hatred. And allow yourselves to be alright with others deliberately choosing for themselves and to be who they are.

You ask, will this lead to a more pure, positive, deliberate life? Absolutely, because people will be able to let their guard down, trip, fall, and get back up, still define themselves without disdain while they Calibrate and Deliberately Create. But the Question BegsAn Answer

WHAT DO YOU WANT?

DESIGN YOUR LIFE AND SEE YOUR SOUL

CHAPTER 16

The Final Checklist:

1. You are a Mental Magnet.
2. Your "Thoughts" Create Things beyond **"What Is"**.
3. Desire with passion and do what you love.
4. Believe that it is yours and there is no failure.
5. Visualize until it materializes.
6. **Act As If** …Pretend
7. Stay focused and clear on positive desires.
8. Expect whatever you desire and take the action necessary.
9. Be proactive and not reactive
10. Be Grateful and have Faith before you receive.
11. The Law of Attraction, **I Am**…
12. Mindfulness, you are responsible for every choice, what are you aware of?

I AM That
Which I Say, I Am!

BECAUSE IT CAN BE
AND SO IT IS!

Ehryck F. Gilmore, CH

Is a Certified Hypnotherapist, Life Coach, Reiki Practitioner, Empowerment Coach and Intuitive Counselor. He has studied at the Omega Center in Rhinebeck, New York, attended DePaul University, The Chicago School of Professional Psychology and the School of Spiritual Psychology of Milwaukee. He is also a master practitioner of Neuro-Linguistic Programming and studied at the NLPInstitute of Chicago.

Today, Ehryck F. Gilmore, CH, lists author and consultant among his credentials, with his current books:

Why Am I Stuck? *(The Science of Releasing Yourself from Being Held A Mental Hostage.)* He is also co-author of **101 Great Ways to Success** by SelfGrowth.com.

His consultancy and the "No Hidden Agendas" seminars have helped clients, from coast to coast some as far away as London, UK, and Ireland, achieve success on professional and personal levels through Life Coaching, national seminars, and workshops.

Ehryck resides in the Metropolitan Chicago area and is currently working on his next book If You Can Believe

It You Can Achieve It: The Magic of Your Thoughts, and is planning a national tour, Check the website for Radio-Podcast, television appearances, lectures, workshops, and locations. Visit him on the web: **www.ehryck.com**

Printed in the United States
By Bookmasters